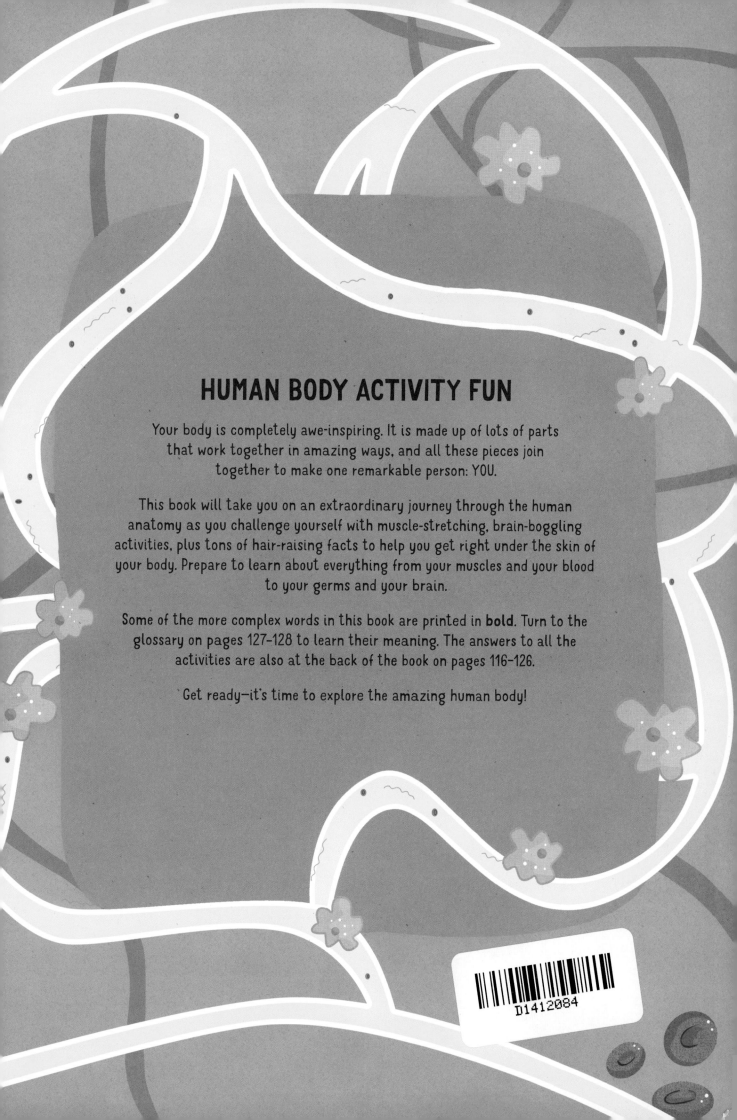

HUMAN BODY ACTIVITY FUN

Your body is completely awe-inspiring. It is made up of lots of parts that work together in amazing ways, and all these pieces join together to make one remarkable person: YOU.

This book will take you on an extraordinary journey through the human anatomy as you challenge yourself with muscle-stretching, brain-boggling activities, plus tons of hair-raising facts to help you get right under the skin of your body. Prepare to learn about everything from your muscles and your blood to your germs and your brain.

Some of the more complex words in this book are printed in **bold**. Turn to the glossary on pages 127–128 to learn their meaning. The answers to all the activities are also at the back of the book on pages 116–126.

Get ready—it's time to explore the amazing human body!

JOINING JOINTS

These images are **X-rays** of different joints. Look at the X-rays and figure out which joints they are. Can you match them to the names on the clipboards below?

A.

B.

There are over 300 joints in the human body, each just the right shape for the job it needs to do.

C.

1.

ANKLE

2.

ELBOW

3.

KNUCKLES

4.

SHOULDER

D.

E.

X-RAY
IN USE

Joints that are able to move are called **synovial joints**. They are mostly located in the arms and legs, where movement is especially important. Some joints, like those in the skull where a solid structure is needed, hold the bones tight against each other and don't let them move.

Have you ever wondered why your joints sometimes make a cracking noise? The noise occurs when gases build up in the fluid that surrounds the joint. When the joint is stretched, the gases are released quickly and that makes the "POP!"

F.

G.

5.

WRIST

6.

KNEE

7.

HIP

BACTERIA HUNT

How many green **bacteria** can you find
hiding among the white blood **cells**?

KEY

BACTERIA

WHITE BLOOD
CELLS

White blood cells help defend
the body against infection and
disease. They can engulf
and destroy bacteria.

There can be up to 25,000
white blood cells in a
single drop of blood.

Some white blood cells only
live for a few hours, while
others live for several years.

SUPERHUMAN BODY PARTS

Circle the group below that contains all of the parts you need to make this **prosthetic** leg.

Prosthetics are artificial replacements for people who are missing a part of their body. It is believed that the first prosthetic was a big toe made for an Egyptian noblewoman.

Running blades are special prosthetics created for athletes who are missing part of their legs. The blades store kinetic (active) energy in the same way as a spring, allowing athletes to run and jump. The running blades are lighter than a bag of sugar but stronger than steel.

A.

B.

C.

D.

SUPERMARKET SWEEP

Your digestive system, including your stomach and intestines, breaks down food to release essential **nutrients**. These are then absorbed into the bloodstream. Find the correct path through the supermarket by collecting only the nutrients listed in the key below. Watch out for shoppers blocking your path! How many items are in your basket at the finish?

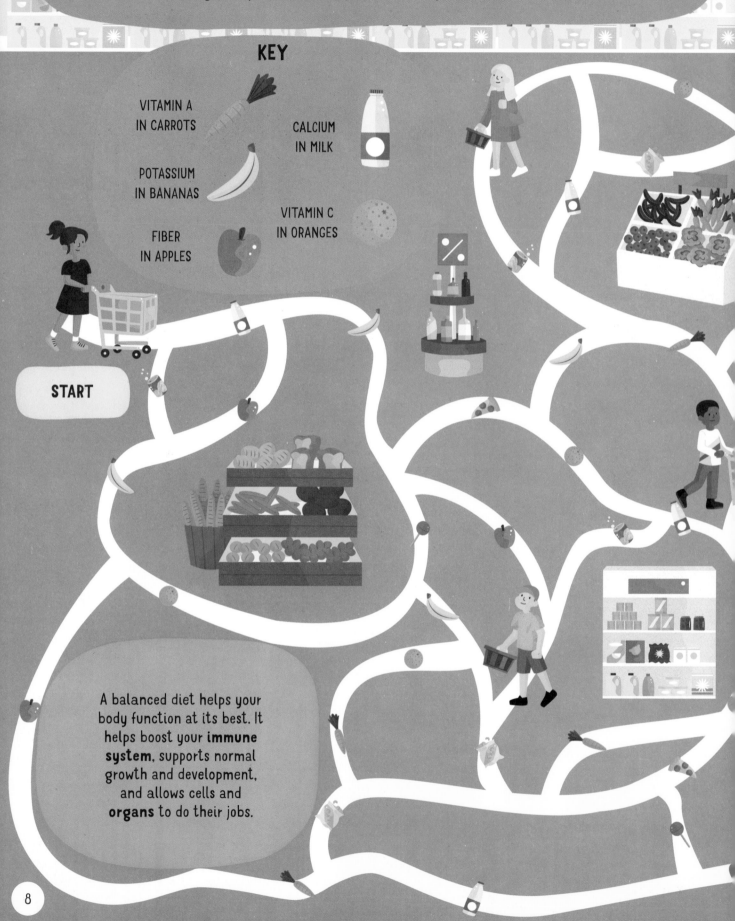

KEY

VITAMIN A
IN CARROTS

CALCIUM
IN MILK

POTASSIUM
IN BANANAS

VITAMIN C
IN ORANGES

FIBER
IN APPLES

START

A balanced diet helps your body function at its best. It helps boost your **immune system**, supports normal growth and development, and allows cells and **organs** to do their jobs.

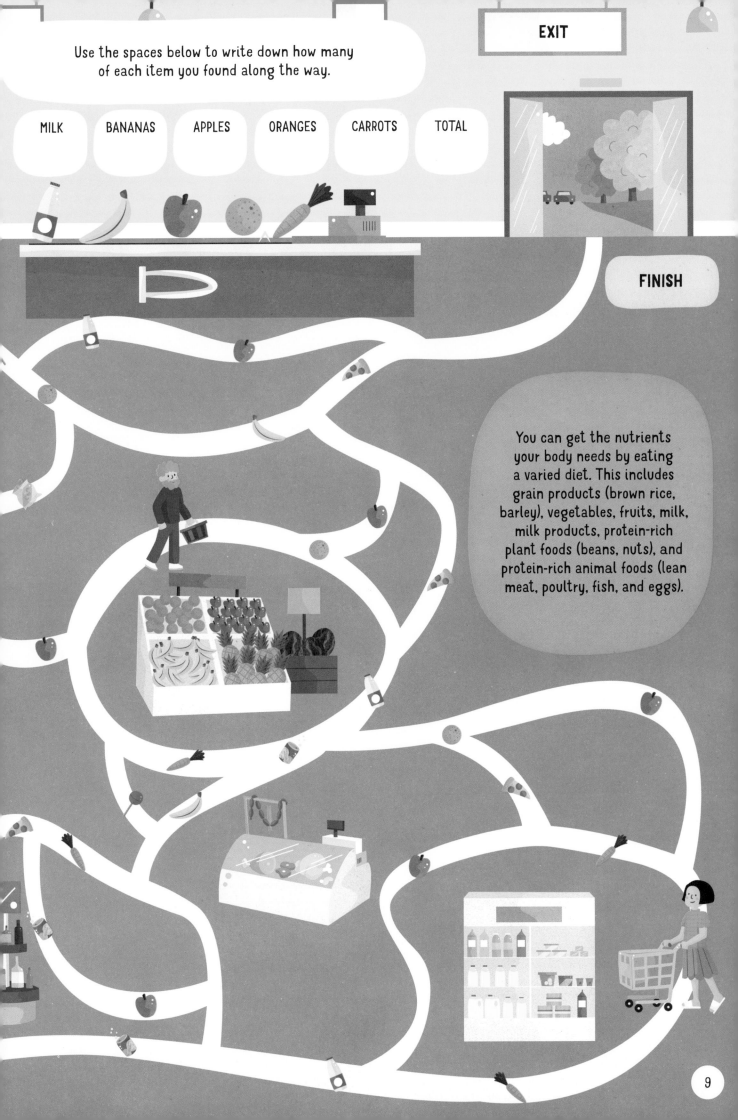

Use the spaces below to write down how many of each item you found along the way.

MILK   BANANAS   APPLES   ORANGES   CARROTS   TOTAL

EXIT

FINISH

You can get the nutrients your body needs by eating a varied diet. This includes grain products (brown rice, barley), vegetables, fruits, milk, milk products, protein-rich plant foods (beans, nuts), and protein-rich animal foods (lean meat, poultry, fish, and eggs).

9

DECIBEL DISCOVERY

Noise is measured in units called **decibels**. Follow the tangled lines to find out how many decibels each of the sounds below makes.

A PIN DROPPING

A THUNDERSTORM

AN AIRPLANE TAKING OFF

AN ALARM CLOCK

A ROCKET LAUNCH

A VACUUM CLEANER

A BALLOON POPPING

Some sounds are so loud they are painful to our ears, while others are so quiet they are hard to hear. Sounds are caused by vibrations. The bigger the size of the vibration, the more energy there is and the louder the sound.

120 DECIBELS

180 DECIBELS

80 DECIBELS

10 DECIBELS

75 DECIBELS

140 DECIBELS

125 DECIBELS

A membrane inside your ear called the eardrum vibrates like an actual drum when sound reaches it. The stronger and louder the waves, the more it vibrates.

MEDICAL MEMORY MUDDLE (PART ONE)

This museum has an exhibition of medical marvels on display. These are medicines, treatments, and scientific discoveries that have been uncovered throughout history. Study the medical discoveries for one minute, then turn the page and see how many of their names you can remember.

STETHOSCOPE

X-RAY IMAGING

PENICILLIN

THERMOMETER

PACEMAKER

VACCINATIONS

ANESTHESIA

DNA

In 1895, a German physicist named Wilhelm Röntgen used X-radiation to see what was going on inside our bodies. The first X-rays Wilhelm took were of metal objects and his wife's hands.

BLOOD TYPES

EPIPEN

KIDNEY TRANSPLANT

ULTRASOUND

Ultrasound creates 3-D images by beaming high-pitched sound waves into the body. These waves bounce off tissues, creating echoes that a computer turns into images.

MEDICAL MEMORY MUDDLE (PART TWO)

Write the names of as many discoveries as possible underneath their pictures.
Try to remember as much as you can without peeking at the previous page.

If you unraveled all the DNA in your body, it would
stretch to the Moon and back 1,500 times . . . or, to put
it another way, to the Sun and back four times!

Your heart's sinus node (located in the upper-right chamber of the heart) is your natural pacemaker. It sends an electrical impulse to make your heart beat. First used in the 1950s, a pacemaker is designed to take over the role of your sinus node if it isn't working properly.

BONUS QUESTION
One picture has changed—can you figure out which one?

PERSONALITY FLOWCHART

What kind of person are you—are you a quiet bookworm or the center of attention? Are you friendly or argumentative? Everyone has a unique personality, which is formed by your **genes** and your upbringing. Use this simple test to reveal more about your personality.

START

YES

NO

Do you think others would describe you as shy?

YES

Do you like exploring unfamiliar places?

NO

Are you scared of what other people might think of you?

YES

NO

Do you like doing things that are a bit dangerous?

Do you get bored easily with new hobbies and keep starting new ones?

Are you sensitive to criticism?

Do you like to be organized?

YES

NO

YES

NO

YES

NO

YES

NO

Extroverts are energized by being around people and are very sociable. They enjoy exciting, sometimes dangerous, things and are good at doing more than one activity at a time.

Thinkers use logic to make decisions. They will weigh all the pros and cons of trying a new or dangerous thing. They like people who are honest and fair.

Perceivers prefer to keep their options open. They often get bored easily with new hobbies and like to be flexible when making plans with friends.

Introverts often work alone or in small groups. They are sometimes described as shy because they prefer a quieter, slower pace of life.

Feelers are sensitive to negative comments. They think about other people and make decisions based on how others will be affected by their actions.

Sensors are very realistic and they like to focus on the facts and details. They apply common sense to past experiences to come up with practical solutions to problems.

Judgers tend to be organized and prepared. They like to make and stick to plans, and are comfortable following the rules.

Intuitives prefer to focus on feelings and instincts. They are very creative and rely on their imagination and ideas, and like to live in the moment.

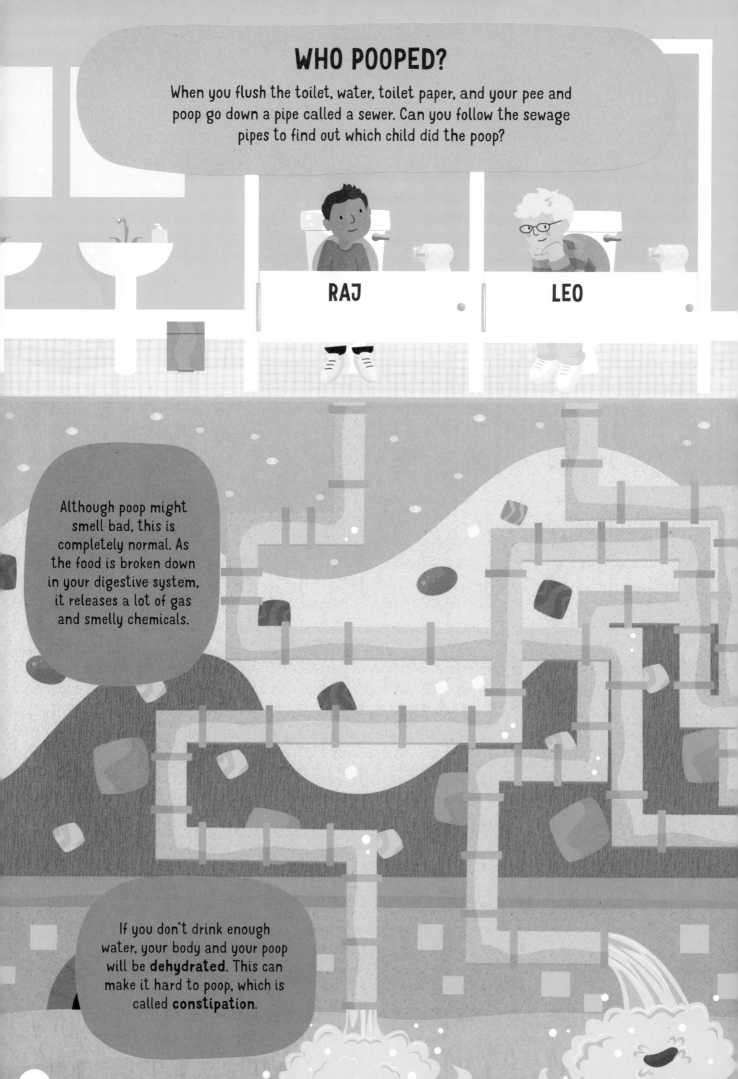

WHO POOPED?

When you flush the toilet, water, toilet paper, and your pee and poop go down a pipe called a sewer. Can you follow the sewage pipes to find out which child did the poop?

RAJ

LEO

Although poop might smell bad, this is completely normal. As the food is broken down in your digestive system, it releases a lot of gas and smelly chemicals.

If you don't drink enough water, your body and your poop will be **dehydrated**. This can make it hard to poop, which is called **constipation**.

ANIMAL SIBLINGS

Humans have a lot in common with animals as certain genes perform the same functions across the animal kingdom. Read the facts about each animal below and guess which ones are true and which ones are false.

1. Ninety percent of the genes in an Abyssinian domestic cat are the same as in humans.

2. Mantis shrimp see color in the same way that humans do.

3. Ring-tailed lemurs are omnivores, like humans. They eat meat and plenty of healthy fruit and vegetables.

4. Whales and dolphins live in human-like families and their brains develop in a similar way to those of humans.

In order to survive, animals need air, water, food, and shelter (protection from predators and the environment). This is the same for humans. Every living thing has its own way of making sure its basic needs are met.

5. Frogs use the energy in their food to keep themselves warm, like humans.

6. Dogs have evolved to mimic human facial expressions in order to get sympathy and attention.

8. The skin tissue and heart valves of pigs can be used in medicine because they are so similar to those in the human body.

7. Koalas have fingerprints that are almost identical to human fingerprints.

In the past, many humans thought of themselves as the only creatures with emotions, morality, and culture. But many scientists now believe that these traits are also found in animals.

GROWING UP

These six children are in a doctor's office. They have had their height measured to see how much they have grown since last year. Read the descriptions below and figure out the height of each child.

1. Nathan is 2 in. shorter than 4'10". How tall is Nathan?

2. Kamal is 4 in. shorter than Nathan. How tall is Kamal?

3. If Vihaan is 1 in. shorter than Nathan, how tall is Vihaan?

The tallest person ever recorded was Robert Wadlow. He was 8'11" tall, which is as tall as an Asian elephant.

4. If Ava is 2 in. shorter than Vihaan, what is her height?

5. Anna and Ava were the same height last year. Ava is now 2 in. taller. How tall is Anna?

6. Marie is 2 in. taller than Anna. How tall is Marie?

SMELLY BINGO

This bedroom is full of smelly items. Search the room for all of the items pictured on the bingo cards on the opposite page. Time yourself to see how quickly you can find them or challenge a friend to a race.

DOG BED | FLOWERS | DIRTY T-SHIRT
ORANGE PEEL | DIRTY SOCK | BANANA PEEL
MUDDY TOWEL | PIZZA BOX | CLEAN LAUNDRY

Humans have around 5 million odor-detecting cells. Dogs have over 220 million of them!

From the outside, it might look like your nose, ears, and mouth are separate, but they are actually all connected inside your head.

APPLE CORE | USED PLATE | TOOTHPASTE
MUDDY SHOES | DIRTY SOCK | SODA
TRASH CAN | HOT CHOCOLATE | LAVENDER PLANT

PICKING SIDES

The brain is divided into two halves. The left side of the brain tends to control logic, such as speaking and writing skills. The right side tends to be more creative and emotional. Can you look at the pictures below and figure out which side of the brain controls them?

The right side of your brain controls the left side of your body, and the left side of your brain controls the right side of your body.

WRITING

SPATIAL AWARENESS

PUZZLES

MATH AND SCIENCE

An adult human brain weighs around 4 pounds, about the same as nine apples.

RIGHT SIDE

ART

SHADOWY SILHOUETTES

Challenge your eyes to the ultimate spotting test.
There are five identical pairs below. Can you find them all?
Draw lines between the silhouettes to pair them up.

Your eye has different cells that help you see in different light levels. Cone cells, for example, help you see color in bright light.

28

The **pupil** is the black hole in the middle of your eye. It gets bigger or smaller depending on the amount of light, so it can stop too much light from entering the eye in bright situations.

Rod cells help you see black-and-white images. They also help you see much better in low light.

STAYING HYDRATED

It's important to consume up to 64 oz of liquid every day through food and drink.
Each square below contains a mathematical equation that will give you the total amount
of liquid in that square. Figure out which squares you need to land on to make
up 64 oz. You can only land on four squares to reach your target.

9 oz + 16 oz

10 oz × 8 oz

4 oz ÷ 2 oz

32 oz - 8 oz

36 oz - 9 oz

32 oz ÷ 2 oz

85 oz - 10 oz

100 oz ÷ 4 oz

64 oz - 10 oz

15 oz + 15 oz

16 oz × 9 oz

7 oz × 4 oz

55 oz ÷ 2 oz

64 oz × 0 oz

8 oz + 8 oz

42 oz - 16 oz

Your bladder is similar to a balloon. It can fill with up to 64 oz of pee before you need to go to the toilet.

About 60 percent of your body is made from water. On average we lose and gain around 64 oz per day. That's the same as about 8 glasses of water.

72 oz – 15 oz

81 oz – 12 oz

26 oz – 10 oz

13 oz – 11 oz

75 oz ÷ 25 oz

120 oz – 25 oz

72 oz – 23 oz

10 oz × 10 oz

12 oz × 5 oz

8 oz × 2 oz

64 oz + 8 oz

8 oz × 8 oz

5 oz × 10 oz

20 oz – 3 oz

80 oz × 1 oz

30 oz × 3 oz

HEAD-SCRATCHING

Head lice are tiny insects that live among human hairs and feed on tiny amounts of blood from the scalp. **Nits** are the empty egg cases attached to hair that head lice hatch from. Look at the key below and count how many head lice and nits are in this child's hair.

KEY

LICE   NIT

It is estimated that over half of all eleven to fourteen-year-olds will get head lice every year. But don't worry! You can get rid of them with a medicated shampoo and a special, thin comb.

Most people with head lice have an average of ten to twenty on their head, but there could be more. And these little critters can move fast for their size, at about 9 inches per minute!

Female head lice can live for up to forty days. Over the course of its life, one head louse can lay up to one hundred eggs.

BODY CLOCK CONUNDRUM

We use clocks to keep us on time each day. But did you know that your body has its own clock? In fact, it has more than one. Look at the clocks below and see if you can figure out what time of day matches to the activities on the opposite page.

A. 6:30 PM

B. 10:30 PM

C. 03:00 AM

D. 8:30 AM

G. 2:00 AM

E. 11:00 AM

F. 2:30 PM

H. 4:00 PM

If you've ever visited a country with a different time zone, you may have found it difficult to go to bed and wake up at your usual time. This is called jet lag. It happens because your body clock is confused.

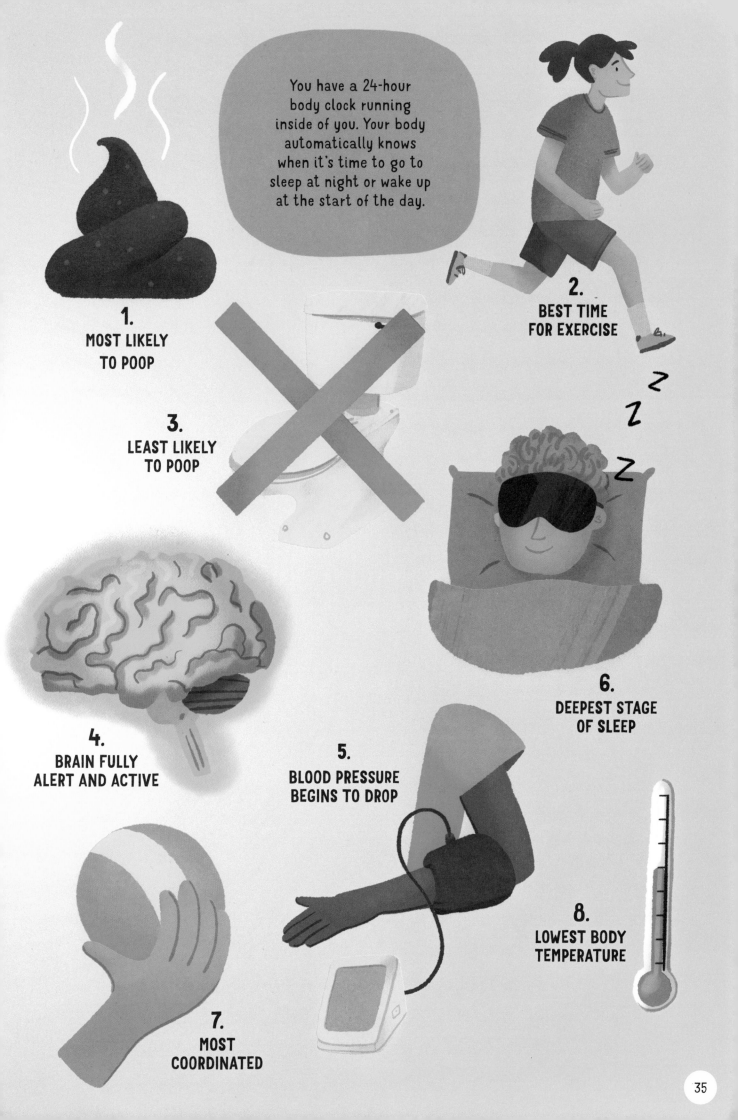

You have a 24-hour body clock running inside of you. Your body automatically knows when it's time to go to sleep at night or wake up at the start of the day.

1.
MOST LIKELY
TO POOP

2.
BEST TIME
FOR EXERCISE

3.
LEAST LIKELY
TO POOP

4.
BRAIN FULLY
ALERT AND ACTIVE

5.
BLOOD PRESSURE
BEGINS TO DROP

6.
DEEPEST STAGE
OF SLEEP

7.
MOST
COORDINATED

8.
LOWEST BODY
TEMPERATURE

REFLEX ROLL

For this game, you will need a marker for each player and a dice. Roll the dice and move your marker clockwise around the board, following the instructions you land on. The winner is the person who gets around the board the most times in five minutes.

You are at the park and a ball is suddenly thrown toward you. Your reflex action means your arm raises to try and catch it. Move forward two spaces.

You accidently put your hand near a flame. Your reflex action causes hot muscles in your arm to pull your the hand out of harm's way. Move forward three spaces.

Reflexes protect your body from things that can cause harm. When you touch something hot, you automatically pull your hand away without really thinking about it. If you fall over, your hands will immediately stretch out to stop your fall.

START

A reflex is an involuntary, or automatic, action that your body does in response to something—without you even having to think about it.

You are cleaning your toothbrush and you push it too far down your throat. You are the same as one-third of the world population who have a weak gag reflex. Move back one space.

You are at the doctor's and they tap the area under your kneecap, but your lower leg stays still. This might indicate a damage to the nervous system. Move back three spaces.

Many reflexes are caused by your **spinal cord** sending messages to your muscles without involving the brain. Other reflexes that we do without thinking include blinking, sneezing, and yawning.

37

TOUCH RECEPTORS

Your skin has receptors in it that detect touch. This helps you react to the environment around you. Look at the pictures below and see if you can match each picture to its correct description at the bottom of the page.

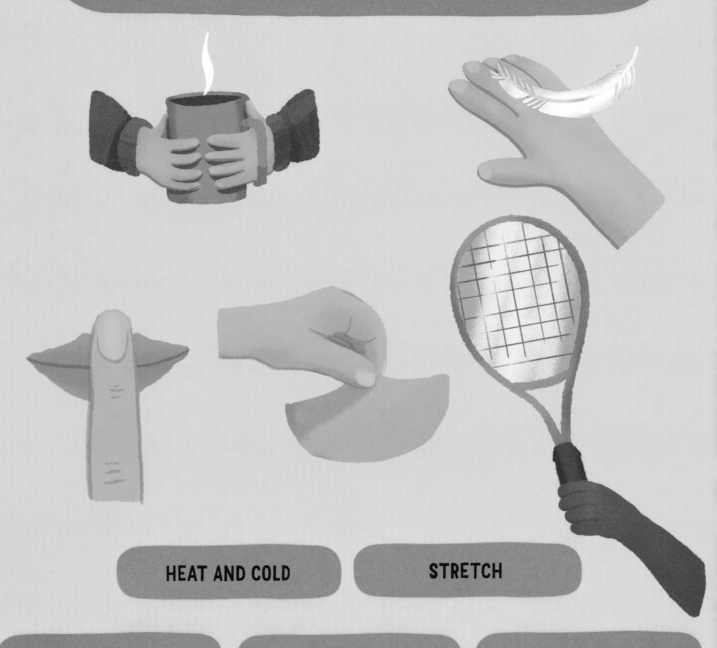

HEAT AND COLD

STRETCH

LIGHT PRESSURE

FAINT TOUCH

DEEP PRESSURE

Your skin receptors react to cold, heat, and pain. An adult has over 4 million pain receptors!

As we get older, we get less information from the touch receptors in our skin. This means that elderly people can hurt themselves more easily.

SOLVE THE SUPER SEQUENCE

Can you complete the three mathematical sequences on the strand of DNA?
Figure out what number comes next and write your answers on the dotted lines.

A.

11

14

17

20

....

DNA is short for deoxyribonucleic acid. Each piece of information is carried on a different section of the DNA. These sections are called genes.

There are about 23,000 genes in the human body. This might sound impressive, but a grain of rice has even more.

B.

2

4

8

16

....

DNA is the material that carries all the information about how a living thing will look and function. For instance, DNA in humans determines what color our eyes are.

The International Space Station holds the DNA of a specially selected group of humans, including British scientist Stephen Hawking.

C.

17

19

23

29

....

BODY SWAP

Can you spot ten differences between these two bodies?

The left lung is slightly smaller than the right because it shares space with the heart. Adult lungs breathe in around 2,375 gallons of air a day. That's enough air to fill over 100,000 balloons.

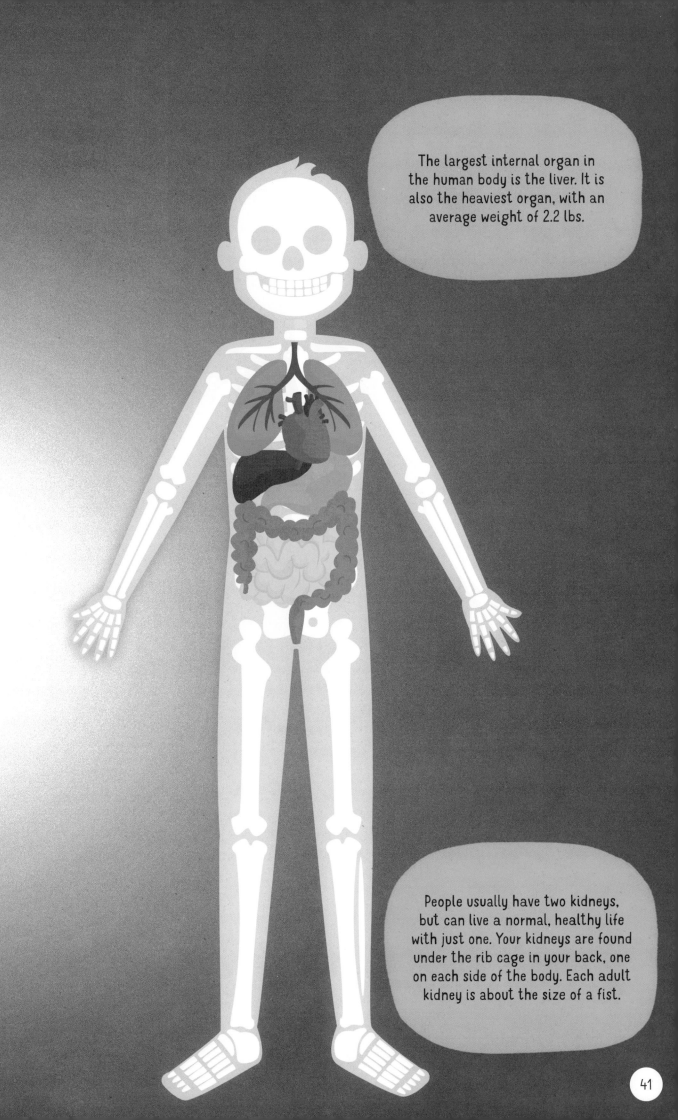

The largest internal organ in the human body is the liver. It is also the heaviest organ, with an average weight of 2.2 lbs.

People usually have two kidneys, but can live a normal, healthy life with just one. Your kidneys are found under the rib cage in your back, one on each side of the body. Each adult kidney is about the size of a fist.

WALK THE LINE

Balance is the ability to maintain a controlled body position while performing a task. This skill is used by tightrope walkers who successfully travel along a thin wire. Read the descriptions next to each tightrope walker below and solve the clues to discover where they are trying to go. Then draw a straight line to help them reach the correct destination.

1.

I'm trying to get to the highest platform in our circus tent.

2.

This balancing pole should help me on my journey to the highest point in the city, on top of a glass building.

3.

I want to see the world upside down from my vantage point at the top of a mountain.

4.

I need to reach a cold and icy peak.

5.

I can't see where I'm going, so I have to be careful not to fall in the rushing water when I get there.

6.

I want to find my way to a high brick wall that is nice and flat, so I don't roll away.

Your inner ear contains fluid that helps it send information to your brain about balance. It is this fluid that can make you feel dizzy after you've been spinning around. Your eyes can see that you have stopped, but the fluid in your ears is still moving, leading to a sense of confusion.

A.

B.

C.

Our sense of balance helps stop us from falling over each time we stand up and move around.

D.

E.

Our brain uses our eyes, ears, muscles, **tendons**, and even touch receptors in our skin to help us balance.

F.

WHAT'S FOR DINNER?

It's time to cook a healthy, balanced meal. Read the recipe cards below and figure out which one uses all the ingredients shown on the opposite page. There is a key placed at the bottom of the page to show you what the ingredients look like.

RECIPE 1
1 burger bun
4 slices of tomato
5 slices of avocado
1 bunch of cilantro
1 slice of cheese
1 lettuce leaf
black beans

RECIPE 2
1 burger bun
1 bunch of cilantro
mashed sweet potato
black beans
5 slices of avocado
2 slices of cheese
4 slices of tomato

Fruit and vegetables are great sources of **vitamins, minerals,** and fiber. They are an important part of a healthy, balanced diet.

RECIPE 3
mashed sweet potato
black beans
4 lettuce leaves
4 slices of tomato
5 slices of avocado
2 slices of cheese
1 burger bun
1 bunch of cilantro

Leafy green vegetables like lettuce leaves and orange vegetables such as sweet potatoes are full of vitamins. They keep you energized and support your immune system.

KEY

| BURGER BUN | TOMATO | MASHED SWEET POTATO | CILANTRO |
| CHEESE | BLACK BEANS | LETTUCE LEAVES | AVOCADO |

BLOOD COUNT CHALLENGE

There are eight blood types, and some are more common than others. Look at the key below and count up how many of each group you can find.

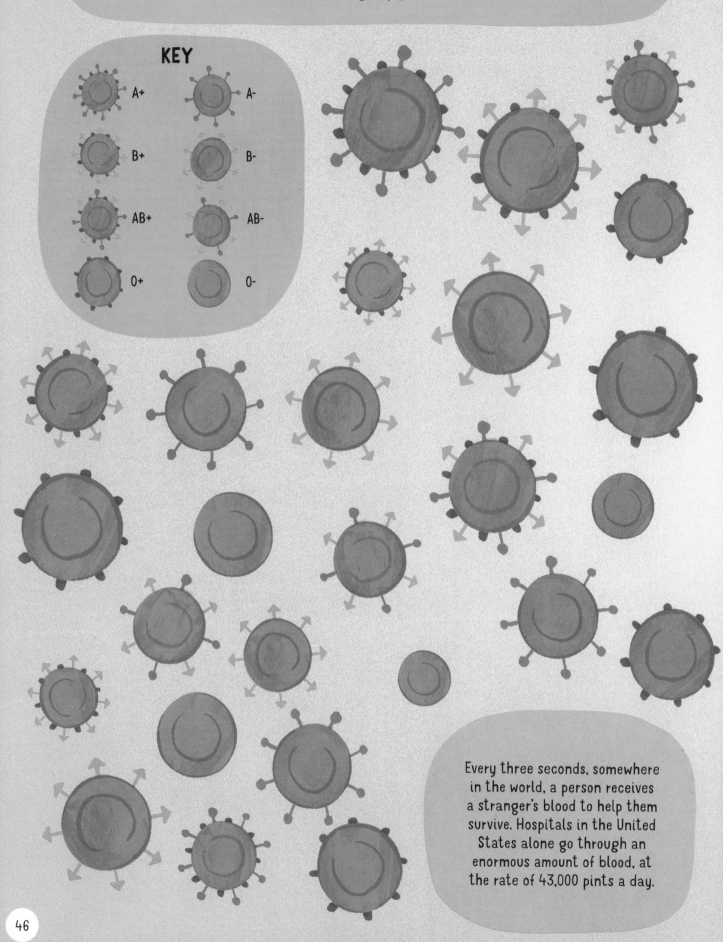

KEY

A+   A-
B+   B-
AB+ AB-
O+   O-

Every three seconds, somewhere in the world, a person receives a stranger's blood to help them survive. Hospitals in the United States alone go through an enormous amount of blood, at the rate of 43,000 pints a day.

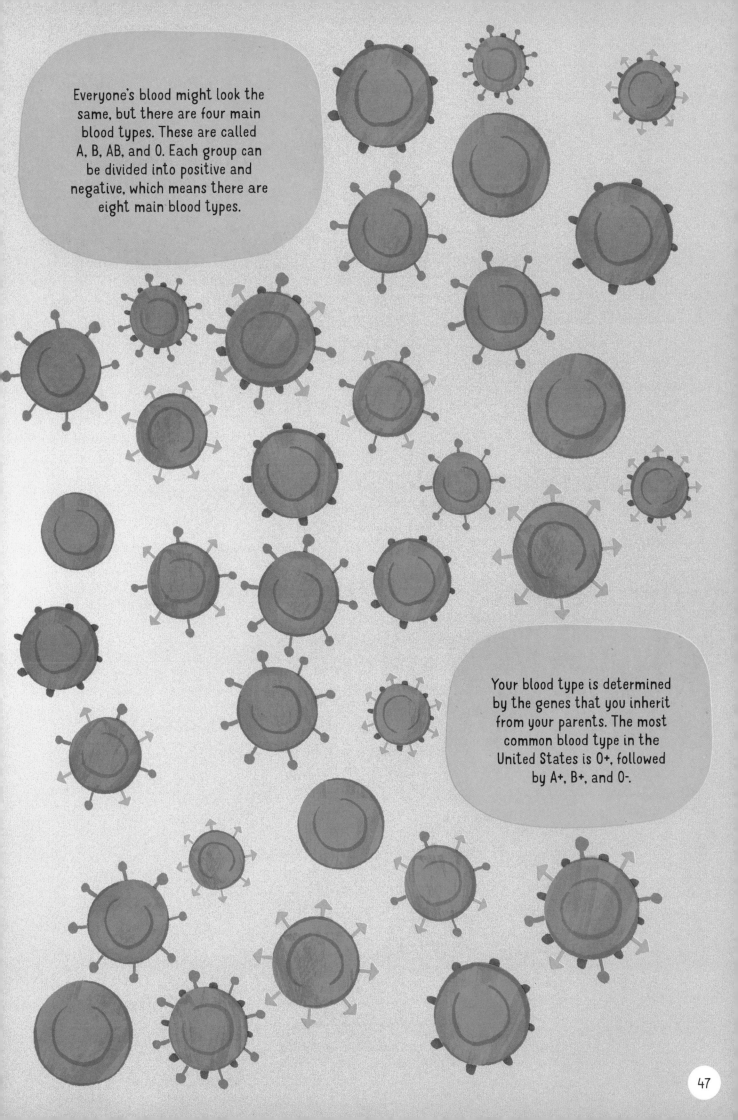

Everyone's blood might look the same, but there are four main blood types. These are called A, B, AB, and O. Each group can be divided into positive and negative, which means there are eight main blood types.

Your blood type is determined by the genes that you inherit from your parents. The most common blood type in the United States is O+, followed by A+, B+, and O-.

POOP PUZZLE

Your poop is created in your large and small intestines. Look at the picture below and figure out which pieces fit in the empty spaces. Can you find the one that doesn't fit?

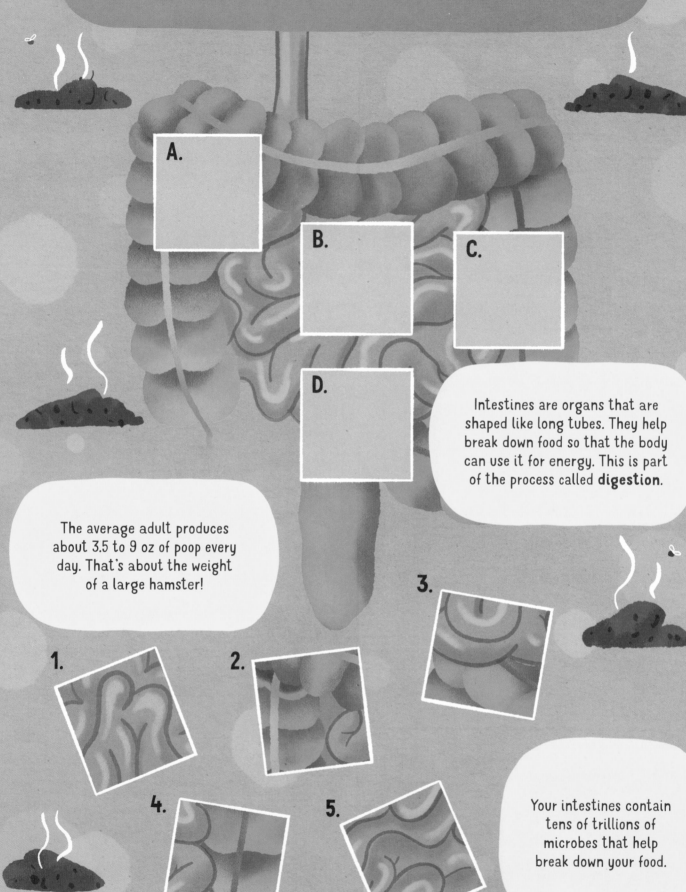

A.

B.

C.

D.

Intestines are organs that are shaped like long tubes. They help break down food so that the body can use it for energy. This is part of the process called **digestion**.

The average adult produces about 3.5 to 9 oz of poop every day. That's about the weight of a large hamster!

3.

1.

2.

4.

5.

Your intestines contain tens of trillions of microbes that help break down your food.

MAKING MEMORIES

Look at the pictures below for one minute and try to remember them all. Then turn the page to test your memory power.

Your memories are not just stored in one part of the brain. A single memory can involve several parts of the brain.

A memory can be reinforced so that you remember it more clearly. Talking about the memory will attach more feelings to it, and looking at a specific photograph will also make the memory stronger.

The record for the longest sequence of objects memorized in one minute is fifty objects. The previous record was still an impressive forty-five objects.

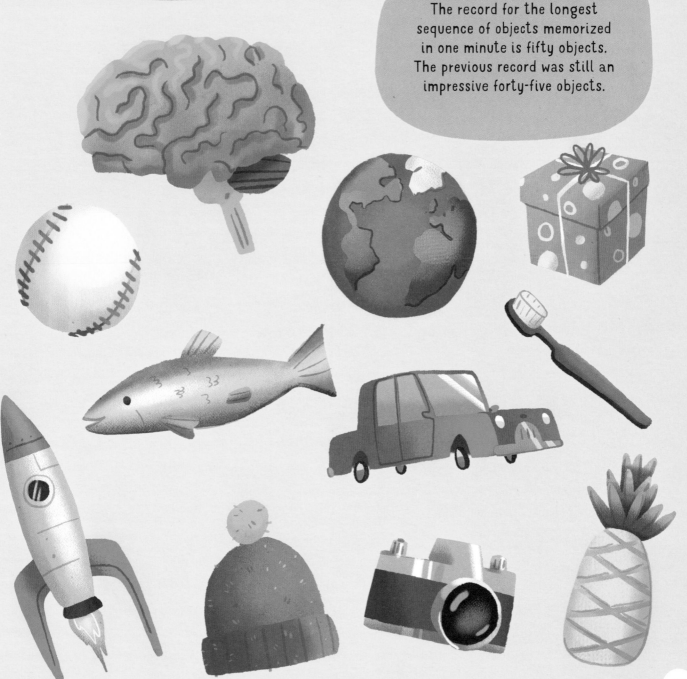

The pictures have been jumbled up, and one has been taken away. Can you figure out which one is missing?

FINGERPRINT MAZE

Can you find the correct way through the fingerprint?

Your fingerprints develop before you are born. Your fingerprints are made of several layers of twisted skin. These ridges of skin make patterns.

There are three different types of fingerprint patterns: loops, whorls, and arches. Everyone's fingerprints are a combination of these patterns.

START

FINISH

PLAYGROUND PUZZLE

After school, this group of friends goes to the playground. This is the most active part of their day. Which tiles at the bottom of the page cannot be found in the picture?

The monkey bars are for more than just hanging around. The grasping action you need to hold on can strengthen the muscles in your arms and hands.

A.

B.

C.

D.

Physical changes happen to your body when you exercise. Your breathing increases to allow more oxygen to get into your bloodstream, and your **heart rate** goes up to get more blood to your muscles.

Exercise that works your heart is called aerobic exercise.

E.

F.

G.

H.

ANCIENT REMEDIES

In ancient times, some strange and scary medical procedures were carried out to try and heal people. Read the statements below and see if you can figure out which are true and which are false.

CROW'S FEATHERS IN WOUNDS

Crow's feathers are good insulators and can keep things warm. They were used by the ancient Greeks to protect wounds, like a bandage. The warmth that the feathers created meant that cuts and wounds healed much faster.

A HOLE IN THE HEAD

The act of trepanation is when a hole is drilled in a living person's head. For a large part of human prehistory, trepanation was performed to treat pain caused by skull trauma or brain diseases.

BLOODLETTING

Leeches are bloodsucking worms. In the past, and even today, they are used by doctors. When they bite the skin, a chemical in their saliva stops blood clots from forming, which can help some wounds heal.

TOENAILS TO REPLACE ROTTEN TEETH

Toenails and teeth are made of the same substance, which made toenails a perfect replacement for rotten teeth. Dentists would bind toenails together and use tree sap to hold them in place.

BARBER SURGEONS

Imagine going to get your hair cut and the hairdresser decides to perform minor surgery on you at the same time. Up until the nineteenth century, hairdressers would offer services such as taking blood and pulling out teeth.

MUD BATHS

Mud baths have been used all across the world. It is believed that the minerals and nutrients in mud can help heal and soothe the skin.

EATING WORMS TO LOSE WEIGHT

Worms eat so much that they have been used to help people lose excess weight. The worms were swallowed whole so that they could feast on the food in the stomach before it was digested.

TEETH TRIVIA

It's time for a trip to the dentist. Four teeth have been labeled below.
Can you match them to the correct type of tooth on the opposite page?

Young children have a set of twenty teeth, called milk teeth. From the age of about six, these teeth will fall out and are replaced by permanent teeth.

Adults can have up to thirty-two teeth. The last four to appear are molars right at the back of the mouth, called wisdom teeth. Not everyone gets these.

A.

B.

C.

D.

1. CANINE
There are four pointed canines that help you grip and tear food.

2. PREMOLAR
The eight premolars are flat and are used to grind and crush your food.

3. MOLAR
The twelve molars are the largest of your teeth and do a similar job to the premolars, grinding and crushing your food.

4. INCISOR
Incisors are like eight little chisels that help you slice your food.

CLASS COMMUNICATION

Body language is defined as the actions and expressions used to communicate with others. This classroom is full of children displaying different emotions through their body language. Can you spot eleven differences in body language between the picture below and the picture on the opposite page?

CELLS SUDOKU

Fill in the two sudoku grids with these six types of cells. Each row, column, and six-square block must only contain one of each type.

1.

2.

CELLS

RED BLOOD CELL

NERVE CELL

FAT CELL

CONE CELL

MUSCLE CELL

SKIN CELL

EXAMPLE:

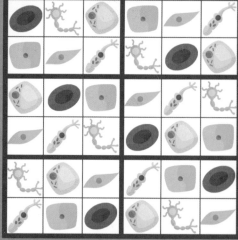

The human body is made of trillions of cells. There are about 200 different types, each with its own size, shape, and contents. Each type of cell has a vital task to help the body function and stay alive. One example is nerve cells, which are long and thin. They carry electrical signals to different parts of the body.

AWESOME EARS

Complete the facts about your ears by filling in the blanks with the correct words from the list at the bottom of the page.

1. The innermost part of your ear is shaped like a _ _ _ _ _ .
2. The **tympanic cavity**, which is the middle section of your ear behind your eardrum, is only slightly larger than a _ _ _ .
3. Ears aren't only for hearing. The fluid in your inner ear also helps with _ _ _ _ _ _ _ _ _ .
4. The ear is actually made of _ _ _ _ _ parts, not just the wrinkly looking flaps on the sides of our heads.
5. Your ears are always switched on and never stop hearing sounds. Your brain just ignores most noises when you are _ _ _ _ _ _ _ _ .
6. The names for some of the parts of your ear are more like the names for things you might find in a workshop, like a _ _ _ _ _ _ _ and an anvil.
7. The middle ear contains three very small bones called **ossicles**. These ossicles are smaller than the size of a _ _ _ _ _ _ _ _ _ .
8. Travel sickness is caused when your _ _ _ _ tell your brain you are moving, but the fluid in your ears remains still. This confusion can make you feel sick.
9. _ _ _ _ contain the smallest bones in your body.
10. Your body makes ear wax to stop things like dirt and dust from getting into your inner ear. This wax is actually a type of _ _ _ _ _ _ .

WORD LIST

GRAPE SEED	EYES
HAMMER	EARS
SNAIL	PEA
BALANCING	SWEAT
THREE	SLEEPING

ALVEOLUS CHALLENGE

One of these pieces doesn't fit in the picture of **alveoli** below. Can you examine them all and figure out which one is the odd one out?

Alveoli are inside your lungs. They are little air sacs that allow oxygen to pass into your body when you breathe in and expel carbon dioxide when you breathe out.

A.

B.

C.

D.

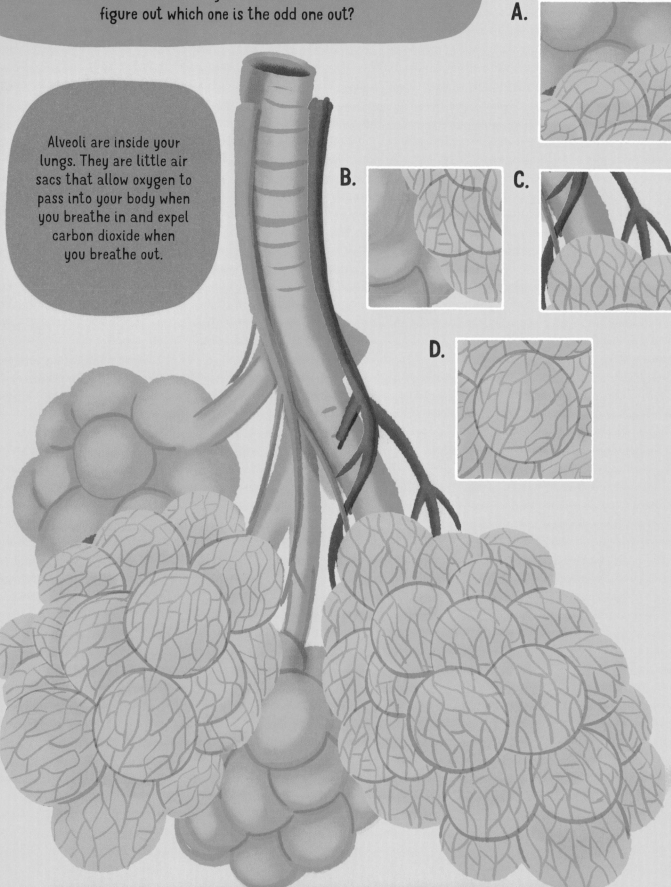

The surface area of your lungs is about 1,100 square feet. This means that a pair of lungs is about the same size as a tennis court.

SEEING IS BELIEVING

Optical illusions occur because your brain is trying to interpret what it sees and make sense of the world around you. Take a look at the four questions below and guess what the answer is. Challenge your friends and family with these too.

An optical illusion is a way of tricking the brain into seeing something that may not be there. Magicians use illusions all the time. In fact, magicians are sometimes referred to as illusionists.

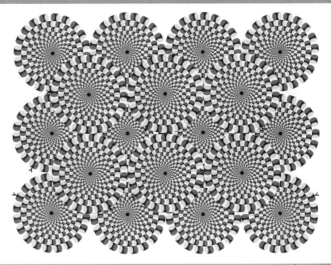

1. Are the snakes moving in this image?

2. Are the horizontal lines sloping or straight?

3. How many legs does this elephant have?

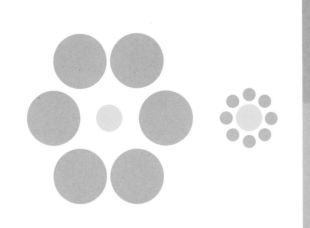

4. Which orange circle in these two patterns is larger?

Look ahead into the distance and bring the tips of your index fingers together slowly in front of your eyes. Keep looking ahead and you'll see a floating sausage between your fingers!

MUSCLE MATH

These heavyweight champions have found themselves in a mathematical muddle. The numbers on their T-shirts show the total sum of the weights that they can lift. Choose the correct weights from the selection below. You can use each weight more than once.

WEIGHTS

12
11
5
9
4
6

EXAMPLE:

12 + 11 + 5

1.

19

2.

14

3.

4.

You have over 600 muscles in your body—your tongue alone has eight muscles.

5.

The largest muscle in the human body is in a rather surprising place . . . your bottom! It is called the gluteus maximus.

Of all the muscles in your body, the muscles that control your eyes are the most active. When you are reading a book as you are now, the muscles in your eyes move about 170 times a minute.

MEALTIME MAYHEM

Most people have three meals a day: breakfast, lunch, and dinner. Can you draw three straight lines on each plate to divide it into four equal portions? Each area needs to contain one of each type of food or drink.

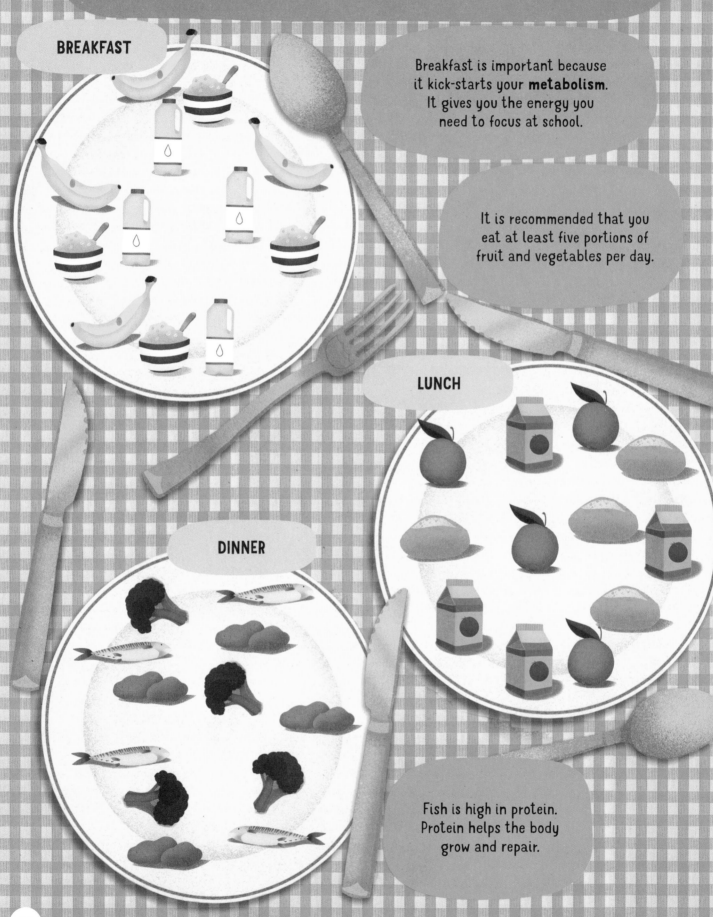

BREAKFAST

Breakfast is important because it kick-starts your **metabolism**. It gives you the energy you need to focus at school.

It is recommended that you eat at least five portions of fruit and vegetables per day.

LUNCH

DINNER

Fish is high in protein. Protein helps the body grow and repair.

X-RAY VISION

Can you spot the five surprising hidden objects in the X-ray below?

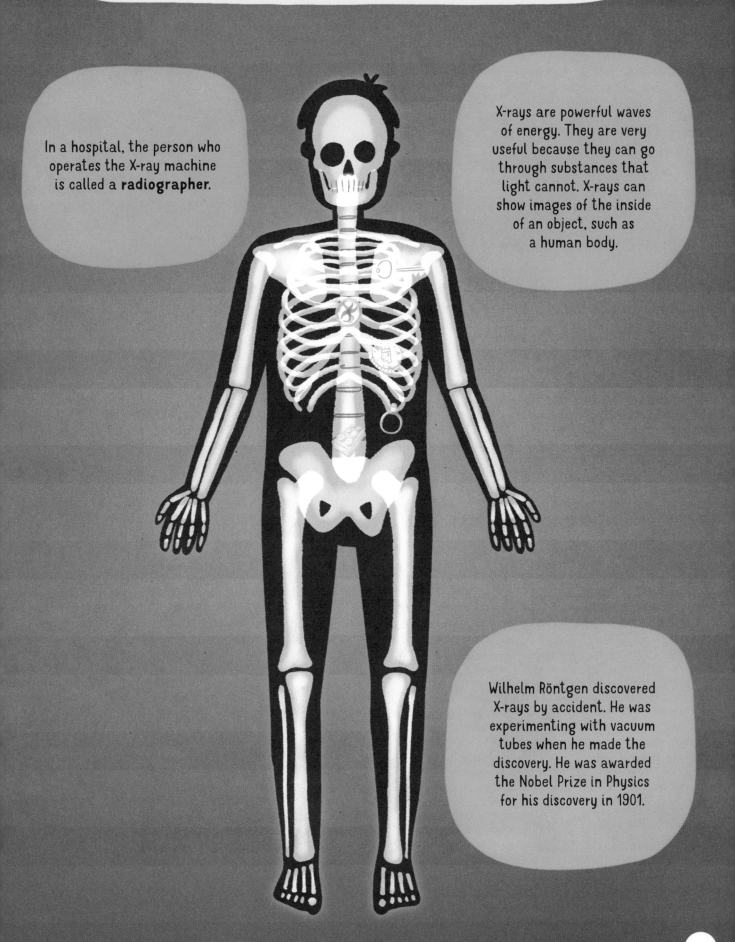

In a hospital, the person who operates the X-ray machine is called a **radiographer**.

X-rays are powerful waves of energy. They are very useful because they can go through substances that light cannot. X-rays can show images of the inside of an object, such as a human body.

Wilhelm Röntgen discovered X-rays by accident. He was experimenting with vacuum tubes when he made the discovery. He was awarded the Nobel Prize in Physics for his discovery in 1901.

ALLERGIES SUDOKU

Fill in the two sudoku grids with these six **allergens**. Each row, column, and six-square block must only contain one of each type.

1.

2.

ALLERGENS

ANIMAL FUR   INSECT STINGS   NUTS

POLLEN   DUST MITES   DAIRY

EXAMPLE:

An **allergy** is when the body's immune system reacts to a normally harmless food or substance.

Common things people are allergic to include pollen (hay fever), nuts, animal fur, and insect stings.

SLEEP MATCH

Everyone needs sleep, and we cannot survive without it—but we don't all need the same amount of it. Match the person to how much sleep they need by drawing a line between them and the correct clock.

NEWBORN BABY

10 HOURS

ADULT

17 HOURS

Scientists are unsure exactly why we yawn—whatever the reason, the average yawn lasts six seconds.

SIX-MONTH-OLD BABY

7 HOURS

FIFTEEN-YEAR-OLD

14 HOURS

We spend around a third of our lives sleeping.

EIGHT-YEAR-OLD

9 HOURS

SPOT THE SIBLING

Though some twins look identical, others can look very different from one another. Can you spot the five differences between these twins?

Identical twins don't have completely identical fingerprints. That's because fingerprints don't just depend on your genes.

70

IQ TEST

IQ (intelligence quotient) tests measure intelligence by focusing on short-term memory, problem-solving, mathematical ability, and visual skills. IQ tests include puzzles, which are similar to these four. Can you figure out the answers?

1. Look at the sequence below and figure out what comes next, either A, B, or C.

A. B. C.

2. Here are some calculations using flowers. Can you figure out the number that each flower is worth and then calculate the missing answer below?

3. Can you figure out which piece below fits the hole in the picture?

A. B. C.

D. E.

Your intelligence is a way of telling how easy it is for you to learn new skills and take in knowledge.

The human brain contains 200 billion cells. Half of these cells are **neurons**, which carry signals from the brain to the rest of the body.

4. Look at the sequence below and figure out what comes next, either A, B, or C.

A. B. C.

MACROPHAGE MAZE

Certain white blood cells clean blood by eating old red blood cells. Take these healthy red blood cells through the maze. Don't bump into any blue **macrophages**!

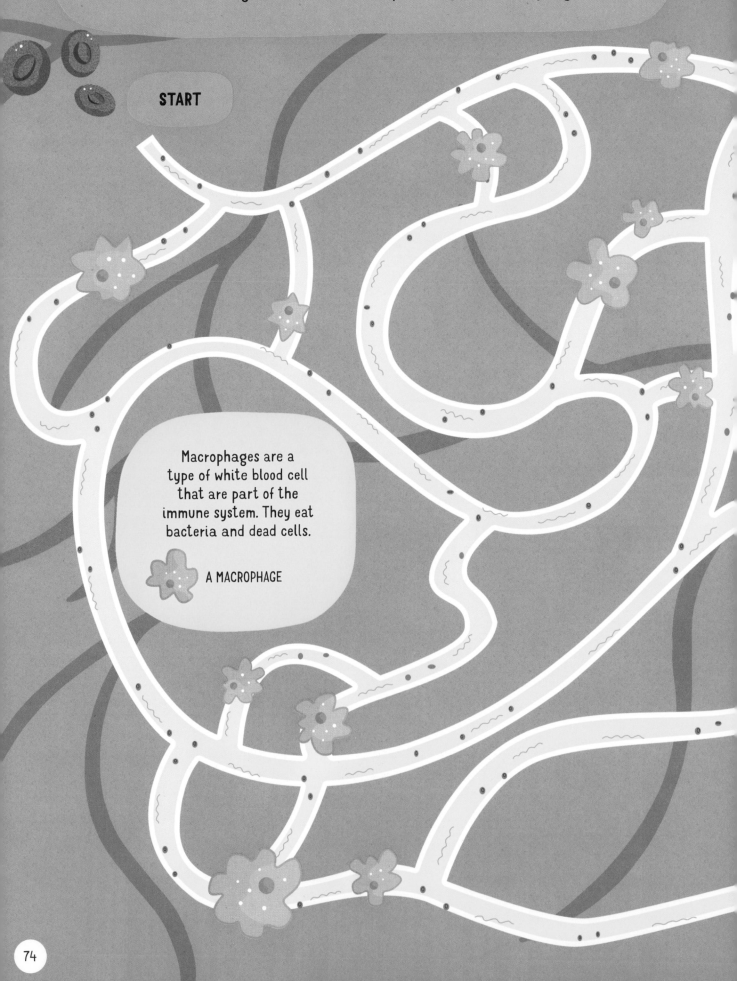

START

Macrophages are a type of white blood cell that are part of the immune system. They eat bacteria and dead cells.

A MACROPHAGE

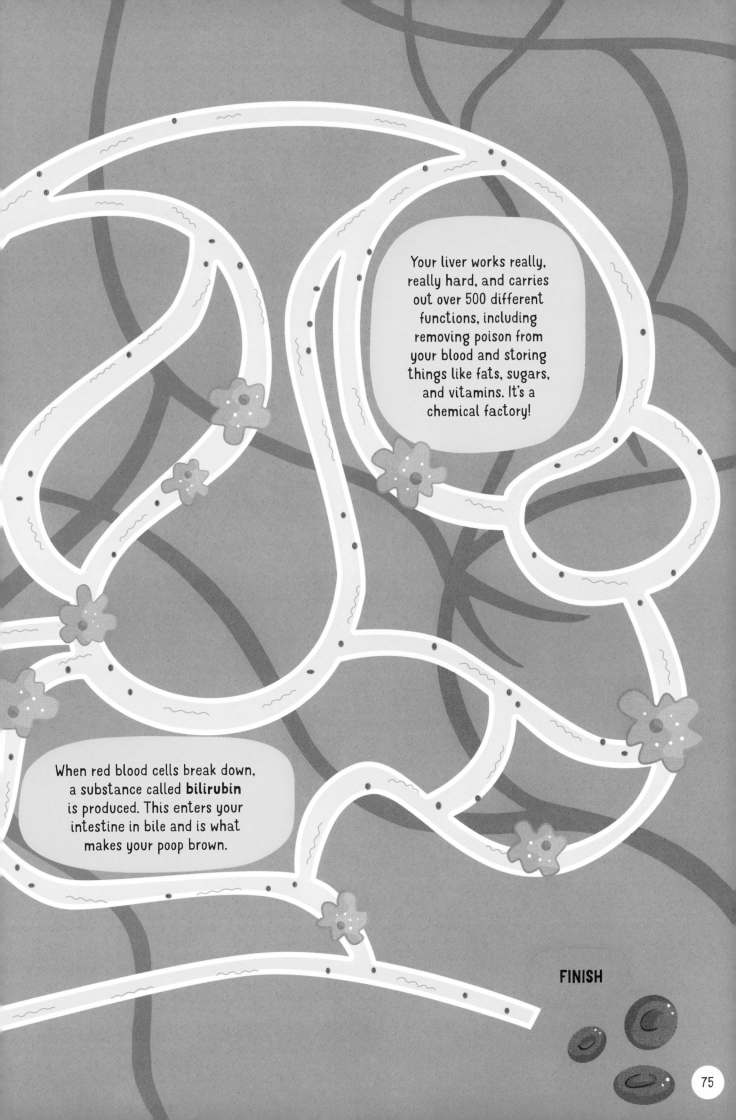

Your liver works really, really hard, and carries out over 500 different functions, including removing poison from your blood and storing things like fats, sugars, and vitamins. It's a chemical factory!

When red blood cells break down, a substance called **bilirubin** is produced. This enters your intestine in bile and is what makes your poop brown.

FINISH

GOOD HYGIENE

It's important to have good hygiene because it prevents the spread of infection and can help you stay healthy. Read each person's completed to-do list below and figure out from the description who has done what on which day of the week. Then fill in each name on the hygiene chart on the opposite page. One name has been filled in to help you.

ARIEL

Wash my hair the day before the school week starts ✓

Moisturize on the first day of the weekend ✓

WALEED

Shower the day after Ariel washes her hair ✓

Buy toothpaste two days after I shower ✓

MAI

Buy soap on the last day before the weekend ✓

Brush my hair three days after Waleed buys toothpaste ✓

JACK

Wash my face the day before Mai brushes her hair ✓

Cut my nails the same day that Ariel moisturizes ✓

LEA

Refill shower gel the day after Waleed showers ✓

Brush my hair on the same day that Mai buys soap ✓

CARLOS

Cut my nails the same day that Waleed showers ✓

Wash my hair two days before Ariel washes her hair ✓

When your body gets hot, it produces sweat, and sweat helps bacteria grow.

Sweat glands are everywhere on your body. The average person has 2.5 million sweat glands.

You should wash your hands with soap regularly, to protect yourself and others from illness. Don't forget to brush your teeth twice a day.

	MONDAY	TUESDAY	WEDNESDAY	THURSDAY	FRIDAY	SATURDAY	SUNDAY
BUY SOAP							
WASH FACE							
BUY TOOTHPASTE							
SHOWER							
WASH HAIR							
REFILL SHOWER GEL							
BRUSH HAIR							
MOISTURIZE							
CUT NAILS	Carlos						

PULSE MATCHING

Your heart pushes blood through your arteries, causing them to expand and contract in response to the flow of blood. You can feel the expansions and contractions in many places throughout your body where an **artery** passes close to the skin. This is called a pulse, and your pulse changes depending on what you are doing. Can you match the person to their pulse rate?

A.
Luke's resting pulse rate was 60 beats per minute. He then ate breakfast and it increased by 5 beats per minute.

93

B.
Belinda went for a run and her pulse rate was 170 beats per minute. She then stopped to stretch and it dropped by 21 beats per minute.

Depending on your age, your pulse should be somewhere between 60 and 100 beats per minute while you are resting.

75

C.
Suhel was on a bike ride, where his pulse rate was 98 beats per minute. He stopped to take a photo and his pulse rate dropped by 13 beats per minute.

140

D.
Tamrin went swimming in the sea and her pulse rate jumped from 60 beats to 33 more beats per minute.

To check your heart rate, hold your palm upward and with your other hand place your index and middle finger on your wrist below your thumb so that you can feel a throb. This is your pulse.

85

E.
Jonny took part in an obstacle course and his pulse rate was 124 beats per minute. When he stopped his pulse rate went down by 49 beats per minute.

65

F.
Marcus went to a party and danced for an hour. His pulse rate was twice his resting pulse rate of 70 beats per minute.

149

SIZE UP

These seven things are all found in the body. Can you figure out which is the smallest and which is the largest? Label them from 1 to 7, smallest to largest, in the boxes below.

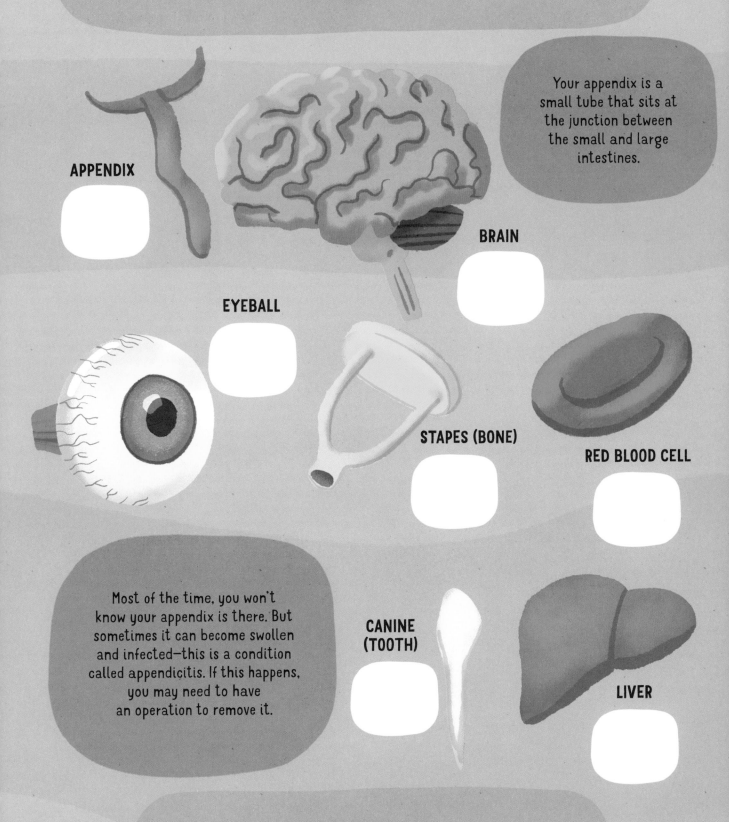

Your appendix is a small tube that sits at the junction between the small and large intestines.

APPENDIX

BRAIN

EYEBALL

STAPES (BONE)

RED BLOOD CELL

Most of the time, you won't know your appendix is there. But sometimes it can become swollen and infected—this is a condition called appendicitis. If this happens, you may need to have an operation to remove it.

CANINE (TOOTH)

LIVER

BONUS QUESTION

About how many red blood cells are there in a drop of blood?

    a. 500   b. 500,000   c. 5 million

FUN AT THE FAIR

Adrenaline is a **hormone** in the body that gives you energy. It can be triggered when you're at a scary or exciting place, such as a theme park. Follow the directions below to navigate yourself around the theme park, then answer the questions about what you see.

DIRECTIONS

1. Start at the entrance in the bottom left-hand corner.
2. Take the left lane and walk past the log ride.
3. Follow the road to the left where you can smell lunch cooking. Look at everyone on the Ferris wheel!
4. Head south. Don't get a fright as you walk past the House of Horrors!
5. Watch out for pirates as you walk toward the hot dog stand and then take a right. Take another right and hear the soothing carousel music.
6. Take the next right and head toward the biggest ride in the theme park.

ENTRANCE

Adrenaline increases your heart rate and sends blood to your muscles so that your body is ready to quickly run away from anything scary.

The release of adrenaline also makes the pupil of the eye larger. This lets in more light to help us see what is happening around us as clearly as possible.

QUESTIONS

1. What rides do you visit on your route?

2. How many children are getting an ice cream?

3. How many food stalls can you see in the entire theme park?

4. What is the child by the roller coaster holding in her hand?

5. How many trees did you pass on your route?

WHERE'S THE PAIR?

Chromosomes are the things that make us what we are. They carry all of the information used to help a cell grow, thrive, and reproduce. The center of nearly every single cell in the body contains twenty-three pairs of chromosomes. These pairs have been split up. Can you help them find their missing half? Both halves will be the same color.

XY CHROMOSOME (MALE)

XX CHROMOSOME (FEMALE)

The twenty-two pairs above look the same in both males and females. The twenty-third pair, the sex chromosomes, differs between males and females. Females have two copies of the X chromosome, while males have one X and one Y chromosome.

Each chromosome is made of a long strand of DNA. It usually looks like a piece of string, but when it is about to divide it becomes an X shape.

SKIN DETECTIVE

Look at the six statements below and see if you can figure out which are true and which are false.

2. The skin is the human body's heaviest organ.

1. We lose about 50,000 skin flakes a minute.

3. Your skin is thickest on your feet and palms.

4. Your skin makes up 32 percent of your body weight.

6. Your skin regenerates itself around every twenty-eight days.

5. The thinnest skin is found on your ear.

ODD SENSE OUT

You have five basic senses that help you understand the world. They tell your brain what's going on outside of your body. Can you find the odd item out in each sense circle?

TASTE

LEMONADE   YOGURT

AVOCADO   LOLLIPOP

PIZZA

LUNCH BOX

TOMATO   CHOCOLATE

HONEY   COFFEE

When it comes to enjoying your food, taste and smell work together. If you hold your nose, you stop tasting your food.

SOUND

VIOLIN   CRYING

TELEPHONE

TRAIN   BARKING

ALARM CLOCK

HAT

DOORBELL

SIRENS

RADIO

There are five main senses—sight, hearing, smell, touch, and taste. The eyes alone contain around 70 percent of your body's sensory receptors.

TOUCH

CACTUS

HAIR

PEN   TENNIS RACKET

CUSHION   RUG
        MOON

DOOR HANDLE   CAT

FEATHER

SIGHT

STARS

BOOK

RADIO WAVES

RAINBOW   LIGHT BULB

TELEVISION   TRAFFIC LIGHTS

OCTOPUS

MONKEY   KEYS

The most sensitive parts of your skin are packed with touch receptors. Your fingertips, lips, and toes are particularly sensitive.

SMELL

SOCKS   CHEESE

FLOWER

PERFUME

LEMON

CAKE   PAIR OF
            GLASSES

TOOTHPASTE

SUNBLOCK

ONIONS

GROUP THE GERMS

Harmful germs sometimes get into our bodies and cause diseases. Look at the key below and count up how many of each germ you can find.

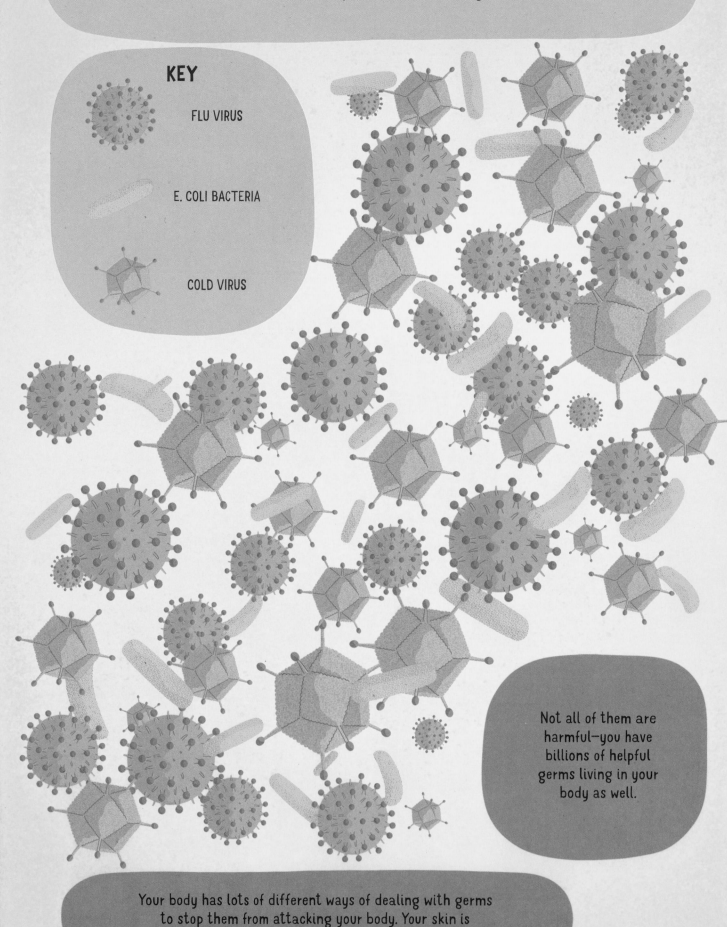

KEY

FLU VIRUS

E. COLI BACTERIA

COLD VIRUS

Not all of them are harmful—you have billions of helpful germs living in your body as well.

Your body has lots of different ways of dealing with germs to stop them from attacking your body. Your skin is a barrier that can stop germs from getting in.

SKELETON DETECTIVE

Look at the six statements about bones below and see
if you can figure out which are true and which are false.

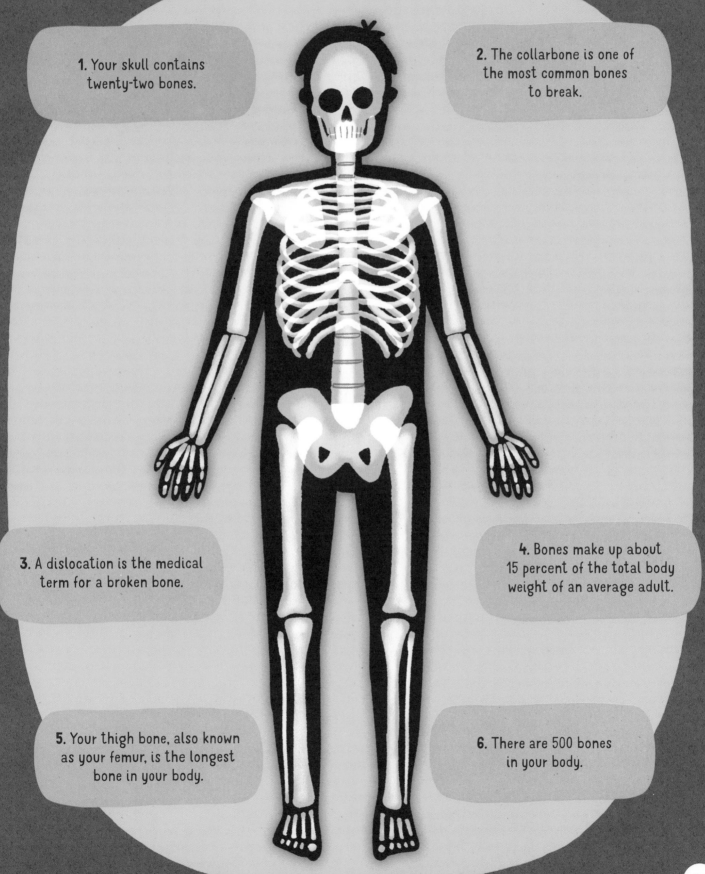

1. Your skull contains twenty-two bones.

2. The collarbone is one of the most common bones to break.

3. A dislocation is the medical term for a broken bone.

4. Bones make up about 15 percent of the total body weight of an average adult.

5. Your thigh bone, also known as your femur, is the longest bone in your body.

6. There are 500 bones in your body.

SCHOOL SPORTS RACE

These four children are having a sack race at a school sports event. Follow the paths to see where each child places.

To stay healthy it is recommended that you are active for one hour every day.

A.

B.

C.

D.

BRAIN-Y MAZE-Y

Can you beat the brain and complete this maze in record time? Write down how long it takes you in the space provided at the bottom of the page.

The brain is extremely sensitive and delicate, so it requires maximum protection. This is provided by the hard bone of the skull and three tough membranes called **meninges**.

Your brain is a fantastic organ. It enables you to think, learn, create, and feel emotions, as well as controlling every blink, breath, and heartbeat.

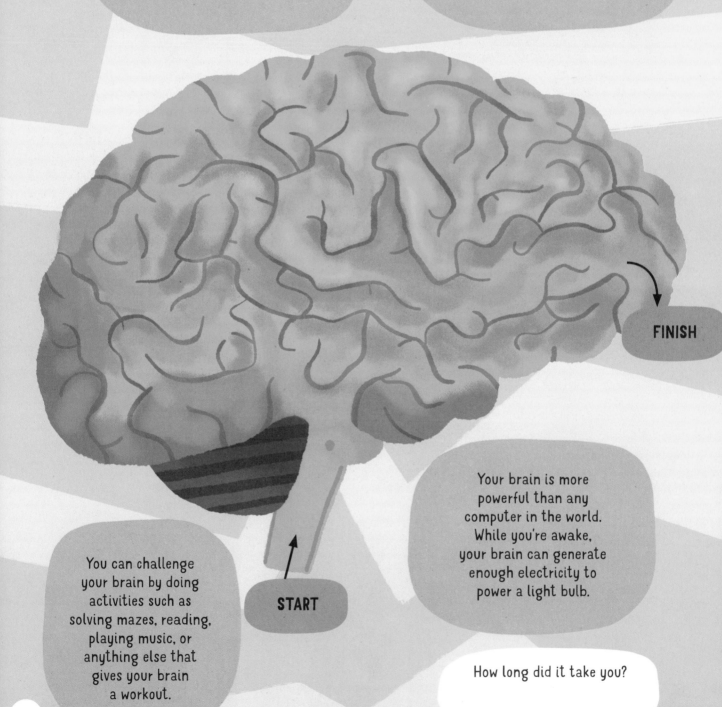

FINISH

You can challenge your brain by doing activities such as solving mazes, reading, playing music, or anything else that gives your brain a workout.

START

Your brain is more powerful than any computer in the world. While you're awake, your brain can generate enough electricity to power a light bulb.

How long did it take you?

....

FINGER FINDING

Match each fingerprint to the correct fingertip. Can you find the fingerprint that doesn't match any fingertip? Fingerprints are flipped when pressed down, so keep that in mind when matching.

No two people have the same fingerprint. Your fingerprints are completely unique.

Fingerprints never change, even when you grow. Fingerprint recognition is a technique used in **biometrics**, a science that uses physical human characteristics to identify people.

Fingerprints help fingers and hands grip things. The tiny ridges help stop objects from sliding out of our hands.

B.

C.

A.

1.

E.

6.

D.

G.

F.

2.

5.

3.

4.

TOPSY-TURVY VISION

Did you know that you actually see upside down? Your brain receives the image upside down, and then flips it around, allowing you to see things the right way up. Can you match each upside-down skeleton below to the correct skeleton on the opposite page?

Each eye contains a small blind spot where the **optic nerve** passes through from the eye to the brain. Our brains use information from one eye to fill in the vision gap in the other eye so the gaps are not noticeable.

The colored part of your eye is called the iris. The black dot in the middle is called your pupil and is actually a hole. Light goes through this, all the way to the back of your eyeball.

PICKING BOOGERS

Boogers are made from dried-out mucus that trap **viruses**, dirt, dust, and pollen. Find all the trapped items from the checklist below, and then add up your answer. Does your total match the one shown?

CHECKLIST

MUCUS

VIRUS

DIRT

DUST

POLLEN

TOTAL = 54

Your nose has two nostrils that allow smells and odors to enter the body. Your nose can detect one trillion smells.

Boogers actually have a really important job. Your mucus helps trap germs and stops them from entering your body. The average nose produces around a cup of mucus each day.

You have 40 million tiny, smell-detecting hairs, called **cilia**, in your nose.

HEALTHY HEART

Complete the facts about your heart by filling the blanks with
the correct words from the list at the bottom of the page.

1. Your heart is about the size of your _ _ _ _ .
2. The average human heart pumps about four to five liters of blood per _ _ _ _ _ _ _ .
3. Your heart is made of two very powerful _ _ _ _ _ that work constantly to move blood around your body.
4. Blood can travel from your heart to your big toe in as little as twenty _ _ _ _ _ _ _ _ .
5. Your heart is a _ _ _ _ _ _ , and as it contracts it sends blood around your body.
6. Blood is carried away from your heart by **blood vessels** called arteries, and it's brought back by blood vessels called _ _ _ _ _ .
7. As blood moves through your arteries, it makes them bulge. This creates something called your _ _ _ _ _ and can be used to measure how quickly your blood is moving around your body.
8. Each half of the heart has two _ _ _ _ _ _ _ _ , a smaller upper atrium and a bigger, thicker-walled ventricle.
9. The heart beats around 2.5 billion times in an average _ _ _ _ _ _ _ _ .
10. The valves inside your heart produce a thumping sound that can be heard by something called a _ _ _ _ _ _ _ _ _ _ _ .

WORD LIST

PULSE
FIST
MINUTE
STETHOSCOPE
PUMPS
MUSCLE
VEINS
SECONDS
CHAMBERS
LIFETIME

COLOR CONUNDRUMS

Did you know that men are much more likely to be color-blind than women? Check out these three color-blind tests and see if you can make out the object in the middle.

There are three types of cells that help us see red, green, and blue light. Sometimes a person might not have some of these cells, meaning they can't see certain colors. This is called color blindness.

A.

B.

Around one in ten boys are color-blind, whereas only about one in 200 girls are color-blind.

The most common form of color blindness keeps people from seeing green and red. They might find it hard to tell the difference between reds, yellows, browns, and greens.

C.

PUSH THAT BUTTON

The red button looks very appealing. Can you find the way through the maze so the neuron can pass the message to the brain that you want to press the red button?

Your neurons are special cells that carry messages to your brain in the form of electrical signals called **nerve impulses**.

FINISH

START

If all the neurons in your brain were lined up, they would stretch nearly 600 miles. That's like traveling the distance from Charlotte, NC, to New York, NY.

Neurons communicate using electrical impulses. These impulses can travel at super speeds of 267 miles per hour throughout your body. This is faster than a peregrine falcon, the fastest animal in the world.

EAT YOUR GREENS

Can you make it through these two grids to complete the games? Follow the vegetables and fruits in the order shown in the top panel. You can move across, up, and down but not diagonally.

1.

START

FINISH

2.

START

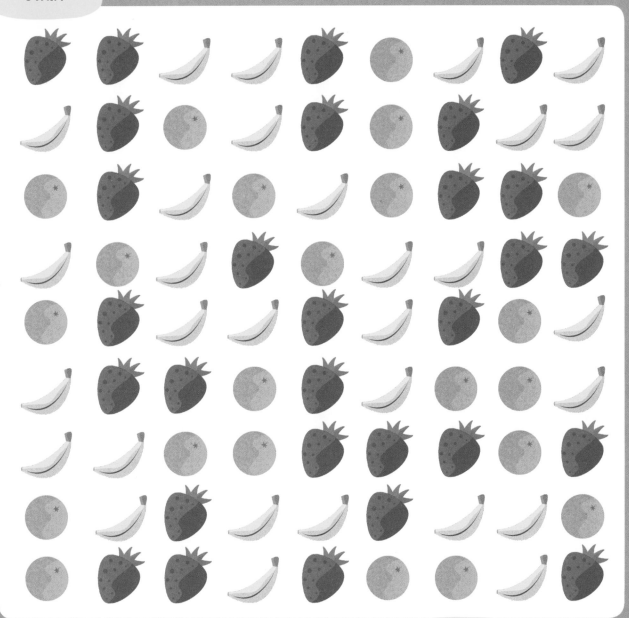

FINISH

Vitamin means "vital for life." Vitamins form an important part of nutrition and are necessary for the healthy functioning of your body.

Vitamin C is found in foods such as citrus fruit, tomatoes, and brussels sprouts. It is important for healthy skin, gums, teeth, and bones.

VOMIT VORTEX

When you vomit, the muscles in your stomach and intestines push food up instead of down and carry that food right back up to your mouth. Can you help the vomit find the correct route out of the body in the maze below?

FINISH

When your body detects something that shouldn't be there, like bacteria or a virus, you might be sick, or vomit.

Acid is produced in your stomach to help break down your food. When you vomit, this comes up into your mouth, together with whatever you've been eating. This is partly why vomit tastes so bad!

START

LAZY BONES

This skeleton is missing some vital bones.
Complete the dot-to-dot puzzle to fill them in.

Over half of your bones are in your hands and feet. Each hand has twenty-seven bones and each foot has twenty-six bones.

If you break a bone, your body takes about twelve weeks to rebuild the broken bone.

Your bones are stronger than concrete and steel but are much lighter.

THINK SMART

There are three pieces missing from the picture below and there are six pieces to choose from. Can you figure out which are the correct three pieces? Look at the pieces from all angles—some pieces may have been rotated.

A.

B.

C.

1.

Lateral thinking is a way of coming up with solutions to problems in a creative way, rather than just coming up with the obvious, logical route.

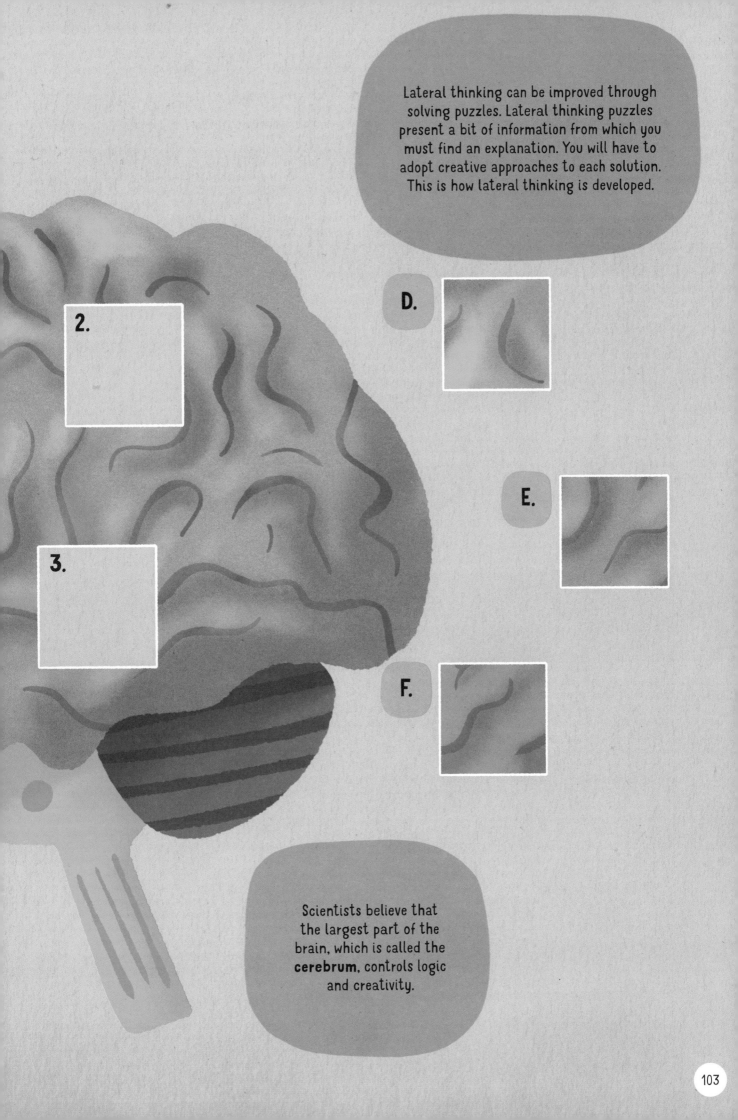

Lateral thinking can be improved through solving puzzles. Lateral thinking puzzles present a bit of information from which you must find an explanation. You will have to adopt creative approaches to each solution. This is how lateral thinking is developed.

D.

2.

E.

3.

F.

Scientists believe that the largest part of the brain, which is called the **cerebrum**, controls logic and creativity.

THE CELL FACTORY

Each of these cells has a different job. Follow the tangled lines to find out where each cell needs to get to.

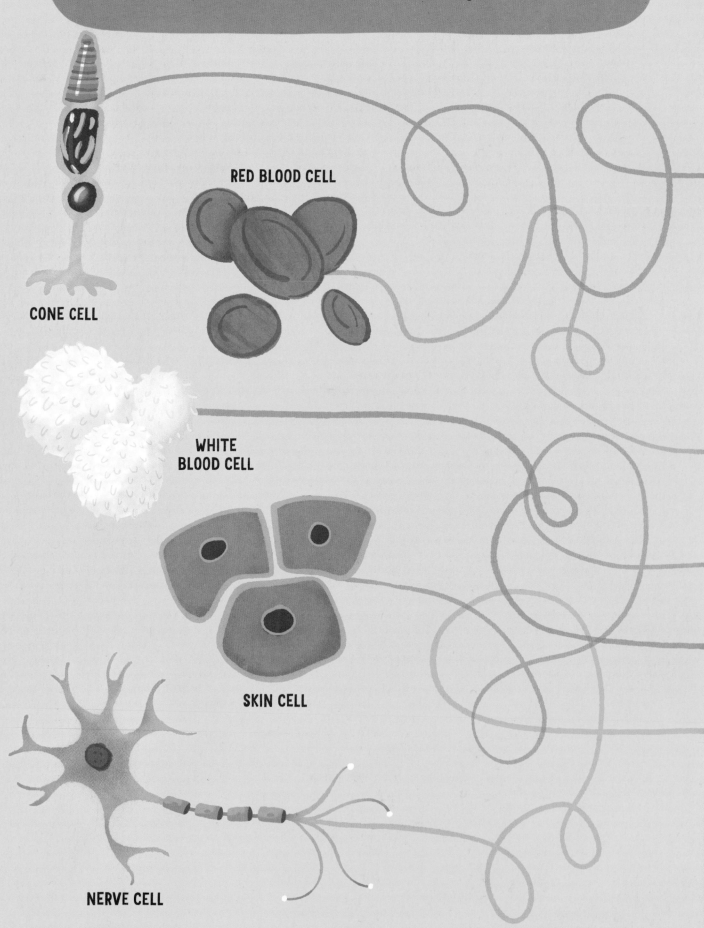

CONE CELL

RED BLOOD CELL

WHITE
BLOOD CELL

SKIN CELL

NERVE CELL

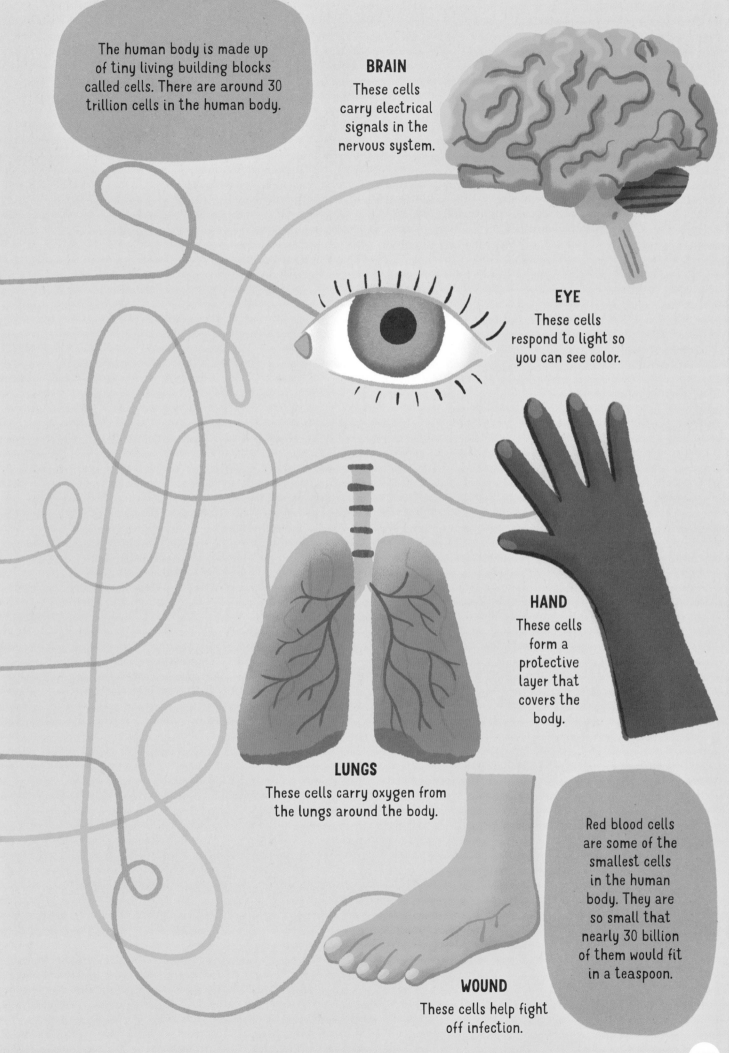

The human body is made up of tiny living building blocks called cells. There are around 30 trillion cells in the human body.

BRAIN
These cells carry electrical signals in the nervous system.

EYE
These cells respond to light so you can see color.

HAND
These cells form a protective layer that covers the body.

LUNGS
These cells carry oxygen from the lungs around the body.

Red blood cells are some of the smallest cells in the human body. They are so small that nearly 30 billion of them would fit in a teaspoon.

WOUND
These cells help fight off infection.

SKELETON SEARCH

Can you draw lines between the bones on the right-hand page and the skeleton below to show where each bone is found in the body?

A baby is born with more bones in its body than an adult. We start with 270 soft bones that eventually fuse together, leaving us with 206 bones as we get older.

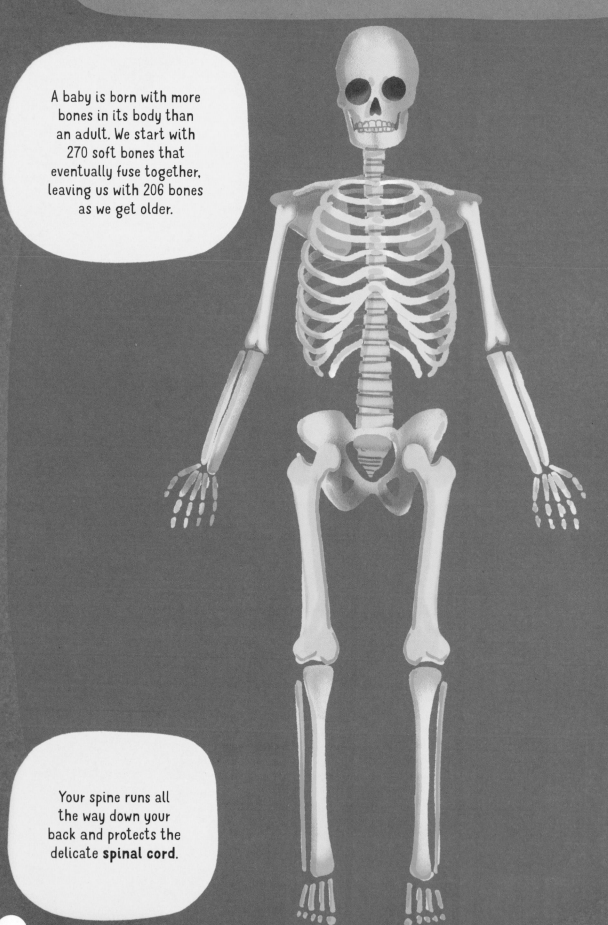

Your spine runs all the way down your back and protects the delicate **spinal cord**.

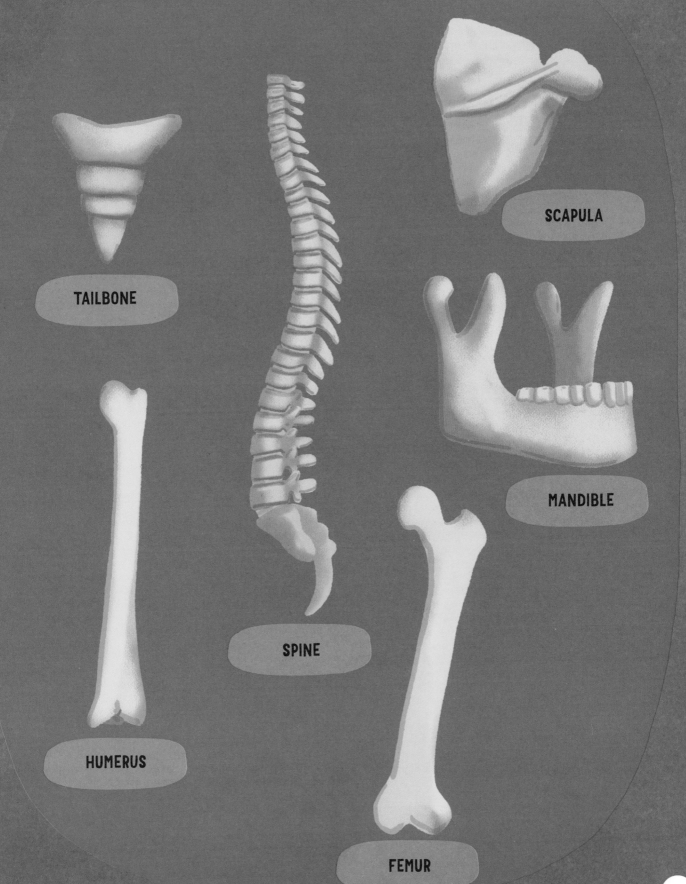

The stapes is a little bone in your ear, and as well as helping you hear, it is the smallest bone in your body.

SCAPULA

TAILBONE

MANDIBLE

SPINE

HUMERUS

FEMUR

LEARN ABOUT LUNGS

Complete the facts about your lungs by filling the gaps with the correct words from the list at the bottom of the page.

1. Every cell in your body needs _ _ _ _ _ _ to function.
2. Lungs are the only human organs that can _ _ _ _ _ on water.
3. You breathe in air that contains oxygen (among other things), and you breathe out _ _ _ _ _ _ _ _ _ _ _ _ _ _.
4. Even when we breathe out, our lungs always retain _ _ _ liter of air in the airways.
5. Your lungs process around 8,000–9,000 liters of air every _ _ _.
6. Your diaphragm is a domed sheet of _ _ _ _ _ _ that helps your lungs shrink and expand.
7. Your lungs are protected by your _ _ _ _ _ _ _.
8. Lungs are part of the _ _ _ _ _ _ _ _ _ _ _ system.
9. In the lungs, oxygen passes from the alveoli into the _ _ _ _ _ _ _ _ _ _ _ in exchange for carbon dioxide.
10. _ _ _ _ _ _ is a type of mucus that is produced in the lungs.

WORD LIST

PHLEGM
DAY
FLOAT
ONE
CARBON DIOXIDE
MUSCLE
RIB CAGE
RESPIRATORY
BLOODSTREAM
OXYGEN

FUNNY BONES

Did you know that you have twenty-seven bones in your hand? Circle the picture below that includes all of the bones that make up this hand.

The fingers and thumb on each hand are made up of fourteen bones, called **phalanges**.

The large number of bones, muscles, and tendons found in our hands means that we can carry out lots of different functions, from lifting heavy objects to more delicate jobs like threading a needle.

A.

B.

C.

D.

TASTE TEST BINGO

This kitchen is full of sweet, salty, sour, bitter, and **umami** (savory) things to eat and drink. Search the kitchen for all of the items pictured on the bingo cards on the opposite page. Time yourself to see how quickly you can find them or challenge a friend to a race.

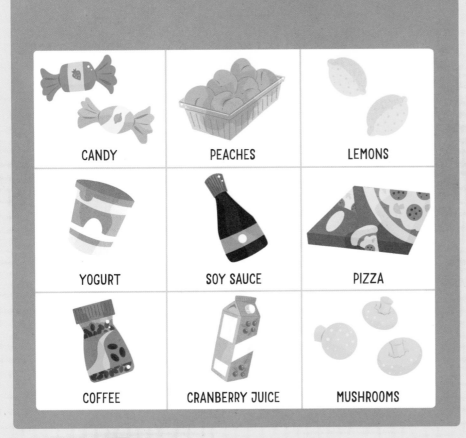

CANDY

PEACHES

LEMONS

YOGURT

SOY SAUCE

PIZZA

COFFEE

CRANBERRY JUICE

MUSHROOMS

Umami describes strong, savory flavors in things like cheese, meat, and fish. It was first scientifically identified at Tokyo Imperial University in 1908.

Your tongue can only actually taste whether a food is sweet, sour, salty, bitter, or savory (umami) when your saliva starts to dissolve the food. Messages are sent to the brain, together with smell information, to identify flavors.

Each person has between 5,000 and 10,000 taste buds, most of which are on the upper surface of the tongue. There are also taste buds across the roof of the mouth and in the throat.

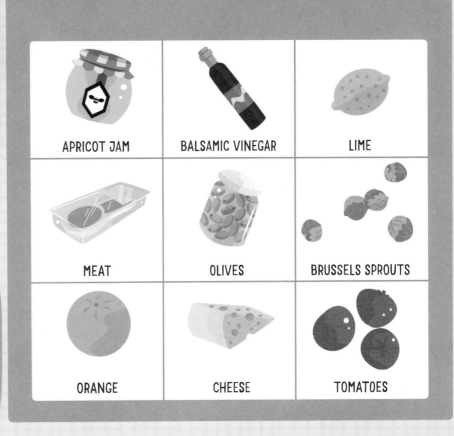

APRICOT JAM

BALSAMIC VINEGAR

LIME

MEAT

OLIVES

BRUSSELS SPROUTS

ORANGE

CHEESE

TOMATOES

PARTY TIME

Our faces can show others how we are feeling. The children at this birthday party are feeling a range of emotions. Can you spot the ten differences between the picture below and the picture on the opposite page?

We are able to express six basic emotions using our faces without saying a word. These are happiness, sadness, fear, surprise, anger, and disgust.

It is possible to experience more than one emotion at the same time. For example, you can be both happy and scared about the first day at a new school.

THE BIG HUMAN BODY QUIZ

1. What does the left side of the brain control?

A. Logic
B. Creativity
C. Emotions

2. What is the largest muscle in the human body?

A. Biceps (arms)
B. Gluteus maximus (bottom)
C. Quadriceps (legs)

3. How many bones are there in an adult human body?

A. 700
B. 520
C. 206

4. Which cells help you see color in bright light?

A. Cone cells
B. Rod cells
C. Nerve cells

5. What taste is umami?

A. Savory
B. Sweet
C. Sour

6. Which of the following is not a good source of calcium?

A. Milk
B. Cheese
C. Carrots

7. What percentage of your body is made up of water?

A. 60 percent
B. 45 percent
C. 20 percent

8. Which is the heaviest internal organ in the human body?

A. Liver
B. Stomach
C. Lung

9. Which of the following is not a blood type?

A. A+
B. B+
C. D-

10. How many milk teeth do young children have?

A. 28
B. 20
C. 32

11. What are chromosomes made of?

A. DNA
B. Carbon dioxide
C. Bone marrow

12. What is the name of the unit used to measure noise?

A. Decibels
B. Kilograms
C. Kelvin

13. Which of the following is not an example of a reflex action?

A. Blinking
B. Sneezing
C. Walking

14. What is the average number of breaths the human body takes every day?

A. 20,000
B. 12,000
C. 52,000

15. How many main senses are there in the human body?

A. Seven
B. Five
C. Two

ALL THE ANSWERS

JOINING JOINTS P4–5

A – 3 (Knuckles)
B – 6 (Knee)
C – 7 (Hip)
D – 4 (Shoulder)
E – 5 (Wrist)
F – 2 (Elbow)
G – 1 (Ankle)

BACTERIA HUNT P6

21 green bacteria are hiding in the scene.

SUPERHUMAN BODY PARTS P7

Group B contains all the correct parts.

SUPERMARKET SWEEP P8–9

There are **28** items.

5 milk
5 bananas
6 apples
7 oranges
5 carrots

DECIBEL DISCOVERY P10–11

A pin dropping – **10 decibels**
A thunderstorm – **120 decibels**
An airplane taking off – **140 decibels**
An alarm clock – **80 decibels**
A rocket launch – **180 decibels**
A vacuum cleaner – **75 decibels**
A balloon popping – **125 decibels**

MEDICAL MEMORY MUDDLE P12–15

The **DNA** is facing the other way.

WHO POOPED? P18–19

Lily did the poop.

ANIMAL SIBLINGS P20–21

1. True
2. False
3. True
4. True
5. False
6. True
7. True
8. True

GROWING UP P22–23

1. Nathan is **4'8"**
2. Kamal is **4'4"**
3. Vihaan is **4'7"**
4. Ava is **4'5"**
5. Anna is **4'3"**
6. Marie is **4'5"**

SMELLY BINGO P24–25

STAYING HYDRATED P30–31

32 oz ÷ 2 oz = 16 oz
8 oz + 8 oz = 16 oz
26 oz − 10 oz = 16 oz
8 oz × 2 oz = 16 oz
Total: 64 oz = 8 cups

HEAD-SCRATCHING P32–33

14 head lice
17 nits

BODY CLOCK CONUNDRUM P34–35

A (6:30 PM) – **5** (Blood pressure begins to drop)
B (10:30 PM) – **3** (Least likely to poop)
C (3:00 AM) – **8** (Lowest body temperature)
D (8:30 AM) – **1** (Most likely to poop)
E (11:00 AM) – **4** (Brain fully alert and active)
F (2:30 PM) – **7** (Most coordinated)
G (2:00 AM) – **6** (Deepest stage of sleep)
H (4:00 PM) – **2** (Best time for exercise)

PICKING SIDES P26–27

Left side
Language
Writing
Puzzles
Math and science

Right side
Imagination
Music
Spatial awareness
Art

TOUCH RECEPTORS P38

HEAT AND COLD   STRETCH

LIGHT PRESSURE   FAINT TOUCH   DEEP PRESSURE

SHADOWY SILHOUETTES P28–29

SOLVE THE SUPER SEQUENCE P39

A. 11 14 17 20 **23** (add 3 each time)
B. 2 4 8 16 **32** (multiply previous number by 2)
C. 17 19 23 29 **37** (add 2, 4, 6, 8 and so on)

BODY SWAP P40–41

WALK THE LINE P42–43

1. is trying to reach D
2. is trying to reach C
3. is trying to reach B
4. is trying to reach A
5. is trying to reach F
6. is trying to reach E

WHAT'S FOR DINNER? P44–45

Recipe 3 contains the correct ingredients.

BLOOD COUNT CHALLENGE P46–47

A+	5
A-	10
B+	7
B-	8
AB+	4
AB-	6
O+	11
O-	9

POOP PUZZLE P48

Piece **1** is the odd one out
A – 2
B – 5
C – 4
D – 3

MAKING MEMORIES P49–50

The **camera** is missing.

FINGERPRINT MAZE P51

PLAYGROUND PUZZLE P52–53

Images **A**, **C**, and **H** do not appear in the scene.

ANCIENT REMEDIES P54–55

Crow's feathers in wounds is **false**
A hole in the head is **true**
Bloodletting is **true**
Toenails to replace rotten teeth is **false**
Barber surgeons is **true**
Mud baths is **true**
Eating worms to lose weight is **false**

TEETH TRIVIA P56–57

A – 4
B – 3
C – 2
D – 1

CLASS COMMUNICATION P58–59

CELLS SUDOKU P60

1.

2.

AWESOME EARS P61

1. The innermost part of your ear is shaped like a **SNAIL**.
2. The tympanic cavity, which is the middle section of your ear behind your eardrum, is only slightly larger than a **PEA**.
3. Ears aren't only for hearing. The fluid in your inner ear also helps with **BALANCING**.
4. The ear is actually made of **THREE** parts, not just the wrinkly looking flaps on the sides of our heads.
5. Your ears are always switched on and never stop hearing sounds. Your brain just ignores most noises when you are **SLEEPING**.
6. The names for some of the parts of your ear are more like the names for things you might find in a workshop, like a **HAMMER** and an anvil.
7. The middle ear contains three very small bones called ossicles. These ossicles are smaller than the size of a **GRAPE SEED**.
8. Travel sickness is caused when your **EYES** tell your brain you are moving, but the fluid in your ears remains still. This confusion can make you feel sick.
9. **EARS** contain the smallest bones in your body.
10. Your body makes ear wax to stop things like dirt and dust from getting into your inner ear. This wax is actually a type of **SWEAT**.

ALVEOLUS CHALLENGE P62

The odd one out is **B**.

SEEING IS BELIEVING P63

1. The snakes are **not** moving.
2. All of the lines are **straight**. The black and white blocks are not aligned and so fool your brain into thinking that the lines are sloping.
3. **Four**
4. The orange circles are the **same size**. Your brain can be influenced or tricked by the scale and closeness of other objects in relation to the object being judged.

MUSCLE MATH P64–65

1. 19 = 4 + 6 + 9
2. 14 = 5 + 9
3. 35 = 4 + 5 + 6 + 9 + 11
4. 10 = 4 + 6
5. 23 = 12 + 11

MEALTIME MAYHEM P66

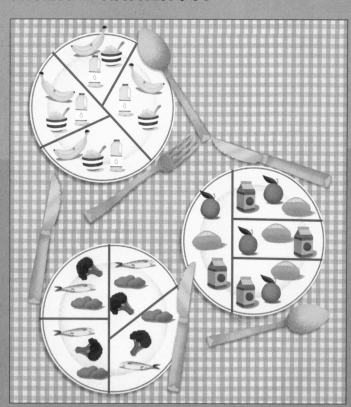

X-RAY VISION P67

The hidden objects are a **key**, a **marble**, a **coin**, a **ring**, and a **piece of Lego**.

ALLERGIES SUDOKU P68

1.

2.

SLEEP MATCH P69

Newborn baby – **17 hours**
Adult – **7 hours**
Six-month-old baby – **14 hours**
Fifteen-year-old – **9 hours**
Eight-year-old – **10 hours**

SPOT THE SIBLING P70–71

Differences:
Hair color
Curly hair
Freckles
Eye color
Gap between teeth

IQ TEST P72–73

1. **B.** It is rotating clockwise.
2. Pink flower = **20**
   Purple flower = **5**
   Yellow flowers = **2**
   Answer = 110
3. **Piece C** fits in the picture. It has the same density of spots.
4. **C.** The pairs of patterns reflect each other.

MACROPHAGE MAZE P74–75

GOOD HYGIENE P76–77

	MONDAY	TUESDAY	WEDNESDAY	THURSDAY	FRIDAY	SATURDAY	SUNDAY
BUY SOAP					Mai		
WASH FACE					Jack		
BUY TOOTHPASTE			Waleed				
SHOWER	Waleed						
WASH HAIR					Carlos		Ariel
REFILL SHOWER GEL		Lea					
BRUSH HAIR					Lea	Mai	
MOISTURIZE						Ariel	
CUT NAILS	Carlos					Jack	

PULSE MATCHING P78

A – 65
B – 149
C – 85
D – 93
E – 75
F – 140

SIZE UP P79

From smallest to largest:
1 – Red blood cell
2 – Stapes (bone)
3 – Appendix
4 – Canine (tooth)
5 – Eyeball
6 – Brain
7 – Liver
Bonus question: C. There are 5 million red blood cells in a single drop of blood.

FUN AT THE FAIR P80–81

1. Log ride, Ferris wheel, haunted house, pirate ship, carousel, roller coaster
2. Five children
3. Four
4. Balloon
5. Ten trees

CHROMOSOME MATCH P82

SKIN DETECTIVE P83

1. True
2. True
3. True
4. False
5. False
6. True

ODD SENSE OUT P84–85

Taste – Lunch box
Sound – Hat
Sight – Radio waves
Touch – Moon
Smell – Pair of glasses

GROUP THE GERMS P86

25 flu virus
26 E. coli bacteria
23 cold virus

SKELETON DETECTIVE P87

1. True
2. True
3. False
4. True
5. True
6. False

SCHOOL SPORTS RACE P88–89

A placed **4th**
B placed **2nd**
C placed **1st**
D placed **3rd**

BRAIN-Y MAZE-Y P90

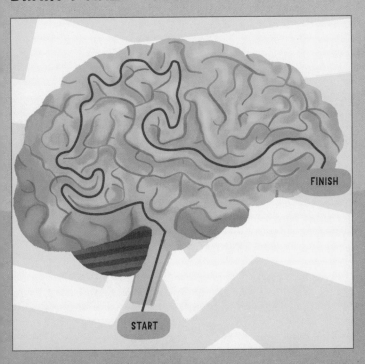

FINGER FINDING P91

A – 2
B – 1
C – 3
D – 4
E is the odd one out.
F – 5
G – 6

TOPSY-TURVY VISION P92–93

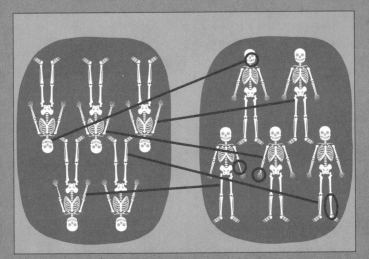

PICKING BOOGERS P94

12 mucus
11 virus
6 dirt
13 dust
12 pollen

HEALTHY HEART P95

1. Your heart is about the size of your **FIST**.
2. The average human heart pumps about four to five liters of blood per **MINUTE**.
3. Your heart is made of two very powerful **PUMPS** that work constantly to move blood around your body.
4. Blood can travel from your heart to your big toe in as little as twenty **SECONDS**.
5. Your heart is a **MUSCLE**, and as it contracts it sends blood around your body.
6. Blood is carried away from your heart by blood vessels called arteries and it's brought back by blood vessels called **VEINS**.
7. As blood moves through your arteries, it makes them bulge. This creates something called your **PULSE** and can be used to measure how quickly your blood is moving around your body.
8. Each half of the heart has two **CHAMBERS**, a smaller upper atrium and a bigger, thicker-walled ventricle.
9. The heart beats around 2.5 billion times in an average **LIFETIME**.
10. The valves inside your heart produce a thumping sound that can be heard by something called a **STETHOSCOPE**.

COLOR CONUNDRUMS P96

A. A rabbit
B. The number 29
C. A star

PUSH THAT BUTTON P97

EAT YOUR GREENS P98–99

VOMIT VORTEX P100

LAZY BONES P101

THE CELL FACTORY P104–105

Cone cell – Eye
Red blood cell – Lungs
White blood cell – Wound
Skin cell – Hand
Nerve cell – Brain

SKELETON SEARCH P106–107

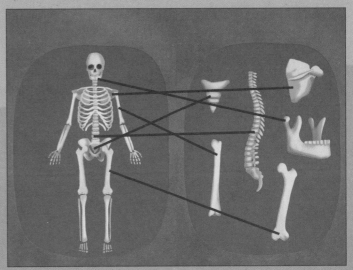

THINK SMART P102–103

Piece **D** fits in space **1**
Piece **C** fits in space **2**
Piece **E** fits in space **3**

LEARN ABOUT LUNGS P108

1. Every cell in your body needs **OXYGEN** to function.
2. Lungs are the only human organs that can **FLOAT** on water.
3. You breathe in air that contains oxygen (among other things), and you breathe out **CARBON DIOXIDE**.
4. Even when we breathe out, our lungs always retain **ONE** liter of air in the airways.
5. Your lungs process around 8,000–9,000 liters of air every **DAY**.
6. Your diaphragm is a domed sheet of **MUSCLE** that helps your lungs shrink and expand.
7. Your lungs are protected by your **RIB CAGE**.
8. Lungs are part of the **RESPIRATORY** system.
9. In the lungs, oxygen passes from the alveoli into the **BLOODSTREAM** in exchange for carbon dioxide.
10. **PHLEGM** is a type of mucus that is produced in the lungs.

FUNNY BONES P109

Group C contains all the correct parts.

PARTY TIME P112–113

TASTE TEST BINGO P110–111

THE BIG HUMAN BODY QUIZ P114–115

1. A – Logic
2. B – Gluteus maximus (bottom)
3. C – 206
4. A – Cone cells
5. A – Savory
6. C – Carrots
7. A – 60 percent
8. A – Liver
9. C – D-
10. B – 20
11. A – DNA
12. A – Decibels
13. C – Walking
14. A – 20,000
15. B – Five

GLOSSARY

Adrenaline
A hormone in the body that gives you energy in times of danger or excitement.

Allergen
A normally harmless substance that is capable of triggering a reaction from your body's immune system.

Allergy
A reaction of the body's immune system to a food or substance that is normally harmless.

Alveolus (plural: Alveoli)
One of the little air sacs inside your lungs that allows oxygen to pass into your body and carbon dioxide to be expelled.

Artery (plural: Arteries)
A blood vessel that carries blood away from your heart to your body's organs and tissues.

Bacteria
Single-celled microorganisms that typically live in organic matter.

Bilirubin
A substance that is produced when red blood cells break down. It is what makes your poop brown.

Biometrics
Science that uses human characteristics to identify people.

Blood vessel
Any tube that carries blood through your body.

Calorie
The unit used to measure the amount of energy in food.

Cell
The smallest living part of your body.

Cerebrum
The largest part of the brain, understood to control logic and creativity.

Chromosome
A strand of DNA found in your body's cells.

Cilia
Tiny hairs in your nose.

Constipation
Having difficulty pooping.

Decibel
The unit used to measure sound.

Dehydrated
Losing more water or fluid than one takes in.

Digestion
The process that breaks your food down so it is small enough for your body to absorb and use.

Genes
Instructions that control the way your body works and develops. They are passed on from parents to their children.

Head lice
A tiny insect that lives on human hair. See also: **Nits**.

Heart rate
The rate at which your heart beats.

Hormone
A chemical produced by your body to change the way different parts of your body work.

Immune system
A collection of cells and tissues that protect the body from disease.

IQ (Intelligence quotient)
The scale on which intelligence is measured.

Macrophage
A type of white blood cell that eats bacteria and dead cells.

Meninges
The three tough membranes that protect the brain and the spinal cord.

Metabolism
The way chemical processes in your body cause food to be used efficiently, such as making new cells and giving you energy.

Minerals
A natural chemical that is needed in your diet to keep your body healthy.

Nerve impulse
An electrical signal carried around your body by neurons.

Nervous system
A special system of nerve cells that controls the body.

Neuron
Also known as a nerve cell. These carry information around your body as electrical signals, known as nerve impulses.

Nits
The empty eggshells that head lice have hatched from.

Nutrients
Basic chemicals that are found in food that your body uses for fuel, growth, and repair.

Optic nerve
The nerve that connects the eye to the brain and transfers visual information.

Organ
A body part that has a particular function, such as your heart or your brain.

Ossicle
A very small bone, especially one of the three small bones inside the tympanic cavity of the ear.

Phalanges
The small bones between one knuckle and the next in your fingers and thumbs.

Prosthetic
An artificial replacement for a body part.

Pupil
The black hole in the middle of your eye, through which light enters.

Radiographer
A person who operates an X-ray machine.

Reflex
A quick, automatic response, such as blinking or moving your hand away from something hot.

Spatial awareness
Knowing where your body is in relation to other objects and people.

Spinal cord
A collection of nerve cells that runs down your spine and connects your brain to the rest of your body.

Synovial joint
A joint that is able to move.

Tendon
Tough connective tissue that links muscles to bones.

Tympanic cavity
The middle section of your ear behind your eardrum.

Umami
The word used to describe a strong, savory flavor.

Virus
A type of germ that invades cells. Viruses cause common colds, measles, and flu.

Vitamin
A substance that is needed in your diet to keep your body healthy.

X-ray
A form of radiation that can be used on humans to see bones.

THE BiG HUMAN BODY BUSY BOOK

Silver Dolphin

ILLUSTRATED BY
RHYS JEFFERYS, GEORGIE FEARNS,
AND MARC PATTENDEN

WRITTEN BY BEN ELCOMB
EDITED BY IMOGEN CURRELL-WILLIAMS
AND HELEN BROWN
DESIGNED BY ZOE BRADLEY
COVER DESIGNED BY JOHN BIGWOOD

WITH SPECIAL THANKS TO
DR. KRISTINA ROUTH

Silver Dolphin

Silver Dolphin Books
An imprint of Printers Row Publishing Group
A division of Readerlink Distribution Services, LLC
10350 Barnes Canyon Road, Suite 100, San Diego, CA 92121
www.silverdolphinbooks.com

Printers Row Publishing Group is a division of Readerlink Distribution Services, LLC.
Silver Dolphin Books is a registered trademark of Readerlink Distribution Services, LLC.

All notations of errors or omissions should be addressed to Silver Dolphin Books Editorial Department at the above address.

ISBN: 978-1-64517-319-9

Manufactured, printed, and assembled in Shaoguan, China.
First printing, March 2020. SL/03/20

24 23 22 21 20 1 2 3 4 5